SINGLES IN THE NINETIES

ANNE FITZPATRICK

BLACKWATER PRESS

Editor: Brendan O'Brien

Layout & Design: M & J Graphics

© Anne Fitzpatrick 1998

First published in 1998
by Blackwater Press,
Unit 7/8, Broomhill Business Park,
Tallaght,
Dublin 24

Printed at the press of the publishers.

Cover Design: Liz Murhpy
Cover Illustration: Olivia Golden
ISBN: 0 86121 963 5

All rights reserved. No part of this publication may be reproduced, stored in a retrieval system, or transmitted in any form, or by any means, electronic, mechanical, photocopying, recording, or otherwise, without the prior permission of the publishers.

This book is sold subject to the conditions that it shall not, by way of trade or otherwise, be lent, re-sold, hired out or otherwise circulated without the publisher's prior consent in any form of binding or cover other than that in which it is published and without a similar condition including this condition being imposed on the subsequent purchaser.

CONTENTS

	Acknowledgements	4
	Introduction	5
Chapter 1	The Joys of Being Single	9
Chapter 2	The Downside of Being Single	22
Chapter 3	What Do Women Look For in a Man?	34
Chapter 4	What Do Men Look For in a Woman?	45
Chapter 5	Drink	55
Chapter 6	Meeting a Partner	63
Chapter 7	Blind Dates and Dating Agencies	76
Chapter 8	I'll 'Phone you Sometime!	85
Chapter 9	Rules Were Made to Be Broken	93
Chapter 10	Sex – Too Much or Not Enough	103
Chapter 11	The Funniest, Saddest, Most Interesting, Best and Worst Replies to the Questionnaire	117
Chapter 12	One-liners, Chat-up Lines and Quotes on Love and Marriage	137
	Conclusion	143

Acknowledgements

*To my parents, Gus and Maureen,
thank you for always encouraging me
to do my own thing.
To my sisters, Mary, Elizabeth and Monica
and my brother Gussie,
thank you for all the laughs.*

Introduction

Ní mar a shíltear a bhítear. (Peig Sayers)
(Things are not what they seem.)

'So, Anne, where is your man?'
'Look Auntie Seppie, I've told you before – I don't have one.'
'But what age are you now?'
'27.'
'My God girl, isn't it about time you got a man and settled down?'

Can someone please explain what 'settle down' means?
If there is anything worse than the aunties and uncles, it has to be the friends that you meet once a year, at Christmas. Having filled them in about how work is going, you say 'No, I still don't have a boyfriend'. Then they tell you not to worry, he's out there somewhere. Or, worse still, they say 'This guy in work is single; I'll have to get the two of you to meet up sometime'.

But who ever said I wanted to meet anybody? I was very happy living a single life. One day I'd get married, but not right now.

I suppose it was only natural that after a while I began to get paranoid and wonder what was wrong with me. The more I was asked the question, the more deeply I analysed myself. In the end, I convinced myself that these people were right. I should have a boyfriend. There was no reason why I shouldn't have one, was there? Hence, I set about looking for one.

In August 1995 I accompanied a friend, Catherine, to a Singles Ball. I was certain that I was going to meet the man of my dreams there, and live happily ever after.

I spent weeks preparing for the big event and spent a small fortune on every beauty aid on the market. I even tried to stick to one of those 'lose 10 pounds in a week' diets. Needless to say, I didn't lose 10 pounds – if anything I put it on, because I was constantly starving and ended up stuffing my face.

The night got off to a pretty bad start. I felt fat and my hair wouldn't go the way it was supposed to. My make-up was a disaster.

Catherine and I arrived at the hotel just on time. People were being asked to take their places. There were twelve at our table – six men and six women. Conversation was limited to what we worked at and where we lived. Boring, basically. However, once the coffee and mints arrived and the band started, we all relaxed a little.

'Will ya be me bird?'

No, please, somebody pinch me – this cannot be happening to me. I am definitely imagining it. Have I just paid £30 to hear a pathetic chat-up line that I could hear in my local for free?

'Will ya be me bird?' Slowly and unwillingly, I turned to my left to see a vision from hell staring at me. Black monkey suit, blond cropped hair, blue eyes that were badly bloodshot, and a body odour that was a far cry from Calvin Klein Eternity aftershave. Had I just spent the best part of 20 days and 20 nights preparing myself for this creature? My dreams of meeting Mr Right at the social occasion of the year were shattered.

'My name's David – what's yours?' he bellowed into my ear, leaving some excess saliva.

'Anne,' I replied.

All I could think of was all those coffee slices, Time Outs, Kit-Kats and jam doughnuts I had sacrificed for this occasion. Never again.

'Would anybody like a drink?' Catherine asked.

'Excuse me,' I said, as I left with Catherine and headed for the bar.

'Oh, my God, Catherine – what a flop.'

'You think you're bad? The guy beside me has just separated from his wife and, to be honest, I don't blame her – he's a pure and utter eejit.'

'Well, to hell with all our dreams of meeting Mr Right; we might as well just enjoy ourselves and take that pack of eejits for a ride.'

'Yeah, exactly.'

'Well then, why the hell are we buying the drinks? That's their job.'

We took a quick trip to the ladies and returned to our table. My 'bird' man had dozed off to sleep, giving me a chance to eye up any available talent at the other singles table. One drop-dead gorgeous guy was surrounded by at least three girls, all of whom were drooling over him.

A grunt from Mr 'Bird' broke my observation of the surroundings. 'What did you say your name was again?'

'Anne,' I replied.

'Look, Anne, do you fancy breakin' a leg with me?'

'To be honest,' I said, 'I don't.'

'Look,' says he, grabbing a chunk of the huge flabby belly that hung from somewhere in the middle region of his completely overweight body, 'is it this that's turnin' you off?'

That was definitely my cue to laugh, and no sooner had he asked the question than I was in fits.

With that, I felt a tap on my right shoulder and turned to find that a colleague of 'Mr Bird' was standing behind me. A shiver went the whole way down my spine as I anticipated a lecture on the disgraceful way that I had been treating his friend, but lo and behold he very politely asked me out to dance and I accepted.

One hour later the guy had practically moved into my left ear, and I was not one bit impressed. The story unfolded that they were both solicitors making loads of money on the ever-increasing wave of marital breakdown.

When he requested permission to buy me a drink, I ordered one for both Catherine and me. While he was at the bar, I was approached by a nineties version of Tom Jones who could have sold the alcohol that was oozing from his breath, not to mention his backside.

'They should bring back those Ballrooms of Romance – honest to goodness, they were a great way of pickin' up a bird,' he said to me.

As I returned to the table I noticed Catherine sitting forlorn, and guessed that she had had enough. We said our goodbyes to 'Mr Bird', his polite friend and all the others at the table, collected our coats and left.

That night, I sat in the kitchen chatting to my sister Lizzie till the early hours of the morning. She had had a bad night as well – the guy she fancied ended up shifting another girl. So, like most girls when they get together, we discussed men. We discussed what we like about them, what we are attracted to and why we get upset by them.

In the end, I realised that I didn't enjoy the ball because I was too caught up with trying to find a man. Lizzie realised that she didn't get her man because she was chasing him. We all know that there is much more fun in the chase than in the catch. We realised that being single is fun and that we will be married for long enough, so why should we need a partner to make us feel complete?

This got me thinking that there must be other people who feel the same way, and so began my journey into the minds of other single men and women to see how they felt about being 'Single in the Nineties'. I wanted to know if they were constantly questioned by people as to when 'are you going to give us a big day out?'. I also wanted to find out whether guys do actually phone girls when they say they will. Did my nineties version of Tom Jones have a point when he said they should bring back those Ballrooms of Romance? Do chat-up lines work?

Armed with Dictaphones, a couple of friends and I toured the 32 counties of Ireland researching the views of single people. I targeted 17–45-year-olds in pubs, clubs, garages, shopping centres and even coming out of mass! The results are compiled in the following chapters – enjoy!

The Joys of Being Single

Mura gcuirir san earrach, ní bhainfir sa bhfómhar.
(If you don't sow in spring, you won't reap in autumn.)

Why are more and more men and women choosing to remain single? Are people genuinely happy being single? Are they content to go to family functions, dinner parties and weddings alone? Do they mind that Valentine's Day is a 'couples' day'? Do they feel discriminated against when they see 'two for the price of one' holiday deals? Are they constantly being told by older folks and relatives that they will be 'left on the shelf'? Do they cringe at the mention of the 'biological clock'?

With these thoughts in mind, I asked the interviewees: Are you happy being single? If so, why; if not, why not? Of the 430 women who answered the question, 49% were completely happy being single and a further 9% were happy most of the time. 43% of the 445 men who answered the question were completely happy being single, with a further 11% being happy most of the time.

What the men who enjoy being single had to say...

❛ There's no better feeling in the world than being able to hop into your car on a Friday evening with a gang of lads and just take off. If you're caught in a traffic jam and you spot a good-looking bird on the street, you can just lower the window and shout out whatever comment you like at her. If you were with a woman, she'd throw a wobbly and accuse you of being common and sexist, whereas the lads understand that it's innocent fun. With the lads, you can drive as fast as you want and stay in the pub for as long as you want, not to mention that women will want to listen to smoochy music and lower the heater 'cause it's affecting their hair or their make-up. *Do you ever feel lonely without a girl?* At this stage in my life, I'm not ready to settle down. I like girls, but most of the time you don't know where you stand with them. If I feel like a shag I'll simply go out and get one.' *Is it as easy as that?* 'Sure it is – there would be no bad men if there were no bad women. There are plenty of women dying to get a man and satisfy him sexually. We're not living in the dark ages now, my girl. STEPHEN, 33, A SHOP OWNER FROM DUBLIN

No hassle; you can go out with the lads and just do whatever you want. CHRIS, 22, A WAITER FROM LIMERICK

There's nothing more annoying than a girlfriend getting on to you when she catches you eyeing up another girl in a bar.
SEÁN, 25, A SALES REP FROM CORK

Being single in college is very enjoyable – there are so many balls and social events that it would be silly to tie myself down to one girl.
CORMAC, 20, A STUDENT FROM LAOIS

It's much more exciting to meet as many different women as possible. In my view, it's all a necessary part of the education.
CORMAC'S FRIEND, CON

I wouldn't be any other way. There's plenty of fish in the sea, and the more I see of women the better looking they're getting. Those belly tops drive me wild, not to mention the high heels, and nowadays if you buy a woman a drink she's yours for the night. Last weekend I was with three different women and it was heaven. There were no strings attached, on my side of the fence anyhow, and it was great. I was like a free stud roaming in a field of mares. Some of me mates are going out with girls and I'm always telling them what they're missing out on. Unfortunately, it doesn't sway them into the single lane. MARTIN, 24, A PLUMBER FROM SLIGO

The greatest thing about being single is that you never know who you are going to meet. There's always that sense of adventure that if you get invited to a wedding or a party you could end up sitting beside a 'babe'. You can also flirt with whomever you want without the risk of being slaughtered by the other half.
SIMON, A FREELANCE JOURNALIST FROM DUBLIN

Women become dependent on you for lifts home, to collect them if they're working late and to organise tickets for concerts etc.

PAT, 26, A BANK OFFICIAL

Being single nowadays is so enjoyable. It's a lot easier than it was years ago – the supermarkets have dinners for one, the flight offers are now catering for one, and in no time they'll have jumbo seats for one at the cinema.

PAUL, A 36 YEAR OLD SECURITY GUARD FROM MAYO

I'm happy with me pint of Guinness – as I do say, she's dark on bottom and blonde on top and she never gives out to me. I never bother much about women; they're far too complicated for me.

MATTY, 32, A LORRY DRIVER

I enjoy single life because in the back of your mind you're always hoping that if the right girl comes along you'll be ready to sweep her off her feet. I'm an old hand at the dating game now and I believe that there are two types of women – those that are into themselves, and those that are into others.' *Could you expand on that?* 'It's a bit like dogs – there's the vicious ones and the friendly ones. The vicious ones are so afraid that you'll encroach on their territory that you find it a challenge to 'get into their minds' and see what they're really like. But when you do 'get in' you realise that they dig their claws in so deep that there's no escape. Just like the 'into themselves' type of girls – they're so into their looks, their make-up, where they go and what they do. They eventually manage to get you into their way of thinking. Whereas the 'into others/friendly dogs' care about how you feel and how they treat you. They're the genuine ones. Unfortunately, there aren't too many of them around. *Do I detect a note of unhappiness with single life?* Absolutely not – I'm very happy being single. It's a lovely way of life; you get used to it and probably get a bit selfish, but my yacht will float in some day! DERMOT, 37, A CHEF FROM WESTMEATH

You can act the *gabhal*.

JOE, 24, FROM CLARE

You're always waiting on them – they're indecisive. They'll say 'give me five more minutes' and then they'll run upstairs and arrive back down in a different outfit and ask you which one is nicer, and you wouldn't even have taken any notice of the first one. Life is a lot simpler without them.
JOE'S FRIEND

Sometimes it's a bit of a drag, but I'd say it's 60/40 in favour of being single.
DONAL, 23, A BUILDER FROM KILDARE

I wouldn't swap my single life style for anyone. I'm of the Leeson Street era, and I go there every Saturday night without fail. It's always a great laugh, and if you want a woman you can have one. I know the morning-after head wouldn't get me a spot on the Gillette advertisement, but by God you're guaranteed the *craic*. With the lads there's none of the 'when will I see you again' rubbish that girls go on with. Male bonding is a natural thing and an important part of any man's life. Even telling dirty jokes in the company of girls doesn't compare with all-male company.
JOE, 37, A FACTORY MANAGER FROM DUBLIN

Being single means being able to fart and belch without having to excuse yourself, being able to chat up as many women as you like without getting a bollocking, and it's plain old-fashioned FUN. It's always enjoyable. I guess I'm just one of those creatures who'll never settle for just one woman. In fact, I'd be dangerous if I did, 'cause I'd only end up having an affair.
EAMONN, 30, A GARDENER FROM TIPPERARY

You've probably caught me at the worst or best time, depending on the stance you're taking, because I've just come out of a four-year relationship and I haven't felt as happy in 4 years! *Are women that bad?* 'No, I just lost track of where I was at and where I was going. More and more I was beginning to lose touch with my mates, and my Sunday morning golf was ruined because I would have to go to her parents' house for dinner. It's hard to explain exactly what it is, but right now I feel as if a huge weight has been lifted off my shoulders and I won't be rushing into a relationship for a long time.

CIARAN, 36, AN ACCOUNTANT

I can't exactly say what it is, but I guess it's that sense of 'footloose and fancy-free', or 'footless and fancy-free', whichever way you want to put it.

PAUL, 22, A MECHANIC FROM DERRY

Bliss, pure bliss – being able to go out and not come home, or go out and come home with a woman.

TIMMY, 26, A FARMER FROM SLIGO

Not having to explain yourself. Women always want to know exactly what you've been up to, how many pints you had and who exactly you eyed up and for how long. God forbid that you're foolish enough to admit to a woman that you eyed up some other girl, because all you'll get is 'Was she better looking than me? Bet she was skinny', or the infamous 'You don't love me any more' trash! Women are nags, simply and plainly – no insult to you, but they are. Whoever said 'You can't live with them and you can't live without them' got it all wrong, because – read my lips – YOU CAN.

KEN, 36, FROM KERRY, WHO WORKS IN THE FAMILY PUB

I suppose pulling as many women as you can is why I love being single. It's a challenge – a bit like getting the next sale – and I love it.

JACK, 24, A SALES REP FROM MAYO

The fact that women are so wonderful and varied means God, or whoever is up there, meant us to explore and experience as many as we can before we get married. You can have the best of both worlds, and get laid as often as you like when you're single. It's like anything in life – if you don't try them all, you'll never know what you really like. If I didn't try all the spirits and all the different types of beer before I settled on Heineken, I'd always be dying to try them out and it would be niggling at me forever. Until I've explored and experienced all women, I won't be settling with just one woman.

JOHN, 34, A BANK OFFICIAL FROM ROSCOMMON

What the girls who enjoy being single had to say...

You have to compromise in a relationship, which I don't like. There's freedom, independence and being able to make up your own mind when you're single.   JANE, 25, A SALES ASSISTANT FROM LIMERICK

Girls are far happier being single than men, because we do a lot more than men. Men are happy just to go to the local pub and drink, but that would bore me to tears. Most of my friends are single and we have a ball. Last night we were at a fashion show, tonight we've just come from a concert and next weekend we're all heading off to London. I firmly believe that if I was going out with someone they wouldn't be happy doing all those things. In relation to things like Valentine's Day, I think it is over-commercialised. Material expressions of love are not what I'm after.   MAURA, 31, A SALES REP

I love being able to do my own thing. If I was going out with someone there would always be indecision, be it what movie to see or where to go, whereas girls just agree on most things.
SHAUNA, 28, AN ACCOUNTING TECHNICIAN FROM WATERFORD

Men are too unreliable – they'll promise you a dinner and then they'll change their mind at the last minute. I'd love to get married one day, but right now I'd prefer to be single.
MAUREEN, 29, A TEACHER FROM OFFALY

You can come and go as you please; you can leave a party when you feel like it and not have to wait around for him to finish his pint. I think people who settle into serious relationships too young are mad. They become dependent on that person and never know what really makes them happy. A friend of mine is sitting in tonight because her boyfriend is in Wales at the rugby match. I think it's pure sad that she can't even enjoy herself without him.
SUZANNE, 26, A FLORIST FROM SLIGO

It's just marvellous. Being single means you can do whatever you want. You don't depend on a man to make you happy or to bring you places. I think it's important that everybody can cope with singlehood. I'm not saying 'cope' as in cope with a problem, because singlehood is definitely not a problem. On the contrary, singlehood is a necessary part of life. It's essential for human beings to be able to satisfy themselves with themselves, that they can realise what really makes them 'tick'. Being single is an adventure, it's fun to get up off your proverbials and do things. It's easy when you know that you have a partner making all the plans on where to go and what to do, but where's the fun in that? The thing I detest most about being in a relationship is having to make an effort with his friends. Bonding with your partner's friends is a tough chore at the best of times, but you also have to be conscious of what you are saying and what they may know about your relationship – mainly wondering whether he has told all the others what you're like in bed.

ANNE, 27, A FARMER FROM WICKLOW

I enjoy being single because you can flirt. Last summer, two of my friends and I were on the town during festival week in Galway and there were loads of drop-dead gorgeous guys hanging out on Quay Street. We decided to pretend that we were French and approached these guys. In our best broken English we asked them where the best pubs in town were. Of course, being Irishmen they fell hook, line and sinker for the French accent. Twenty minutes later, Sophia, Caroline and Zabrine had these guys wrapped around our little fingers. It was a howl. They were even visualising the villas that we lived in in the South of France! When they offered to buy us a second round of drinks we said 'Oh no, you mustn't', and absconded. From there we proceeded to charm another group of guys – this time we were Italian. Well, we never laughed so much. It really was great craic. There's no way on earth that you can have that type of craic when you're going out with someone.

DEIRDRE, 29, A CLERK FROM KILKENNY

I have a lot of friends and love the social life with them. I'm having such a good time that there's no need for a relationship now.

ALISON, 23, A FITNESS INSTRUCTOR FROM WESTMEATH

It's getting easier I think, in the sense that society is slowly but surely realising that it's not everybody's goal to be hitched by the ripe old age of 30. More and more parents are realising that their sons or daughters won't be married at 24 or 25 like they were. They are beginning to realise that single people are right to travel and do all the things their parents couldn't do. I would like to marry one day but at the moment I'm too busy to tend to a man and children. I was accused of being an à la carte feminist last week because I told them in work that I want a real man – not one of these new wimpy types that go hand in hand with the wife to the supermarket. I would hope to hold on to my job until retirement also.

ANNE, 33, FROM MAYO, WHO WORKS IN A HOTEL

Everyone has the potential to be happy with or without a partner, but I think most people don't give themselves the chance. I see a lot of my friends, both male and female, selling themselves short in relationships. They're far too anxious to move in together, and then the real picture gets painted. Some of my female friends would do anything for their partner – their ironing and washing, even. A friend of mine, Paula, has been living with Bill for six months, and was once ordered by Bill not to buy a £6 bottle of moisturising lotion because Bill felt they couldn't afford it, so she didn't – to me that's ludicrous.

CELINE, 33 AN ESTATE AGENT

I enjoy being single because it allows me to explore avenues that I probably wouldn't if I had a partner. Last Christmas, a friend of mine bought me six golf balls because I'm always joking about never finding someone with the right type of balls, as in 'get up and go' – they're either big softies or miserable hard-necks. So I decided to take up pitch and putt, and I've met so many nice people through it. I think being single should be a compulsory part of everybody's life for at least a few years.

RUTH, 34, AN ACCOUNTANT FROM KERRY

At university there is no pressure to become involved with someone, which is brilliant. A gang of us all hang out together, and during rag week we all went through a fair few lads and girls, which is much more fun than just shifting the same person!'

BETH, 20, A SOCIAL SCIENCE STUDENT FROM DUBLIN

It's brilliant craic. You meet loads of men, flirt with the good-looking ones and empathise with the fat and frumpies. A lot of my friends are still single and we have such a hectic social calendar that we wouldn't be able to fit men into it. Who the hell needs them? And it's not that I'm a bitter old hag. I like most men, but at the moment they don't feature high on my agenda.

TINA, 32, FROM CORK, WHO WORKS IN A FOOD PROCESSING PLANT

I can't see myself getting into a serious relationship at such a young age. I enjoy doing things with the girls – lads are not very trustworthy.

TRACEY, 21, A SHOP ASSISTANT FROM LONGFORD

I don't intend to come across brashly, but I hate having to validate my singledom. If I wasn't happy being single I wouldn't be. It's as simple as that. The thing that annoys me most is when people accuse me of being FUSSY. What exactly do they mean – is it that I am looking for a certain type of man, and won't settle for anything less? If that's what they mean, they are spot-on. Why the hell should I go out with someone just for the sake of it? I am an intelligent, attractive, independent and presentable female. I'm not a slapper, and I would not be satisfied with just anybody. I'm a strong-willed individual, and I can live a perfectly fulfilled life without a man. I don't go out looking for a man, because the man for me will find me of his own accord.

PATRICIA, 34, A BOUTIQUE OWNER FROM DUBLIN

My father reckons that every old foot will find a sock, my auntie reckons that my ship hasn't come in yet, and my granny reckons that a spinster's life is nothing to be sneered at. I hate these terms. When are they going to realise that it's not a disease to be single? I got my degree when I was 24 and have only just got an incremental post. Before that I was subbing and barely surviving. Now that

I'm on a decent wage I love spending it on myself. Last month I bought a car, and it is such a wonderful feeling. I'd love children of my own one day, but it's not on my list of 'jobs to do' today. And even if I never meet someone and don't have kids I don't think I'll be too sad, because right now I'm happier than I've ever been.

KATHY, 28, A SECONDARY TEACHER FROM LAOIS

The way society is, you'd think getting a man was more important than securing a job. I'm only 23 and my brother got married at 22 – that was two years ago. Hence, I'm always getting the 'Oh, you'll be left on the shelf' crap from my relations. I'd be the first to admit that a regular shift is nice, but I find that the more people nag at me about not having a fella, the more I never want to have one.

ORLA, 23, A PRODUCTION WORKER FROM DUBLIN

The reason I'm so happy being single is that the best nights I've ever had have been with the girls. When you're in a relationship, the night is pre-planned. You'll more than likely end up back in his house with a cup of coffee that will never be drunk, or in his car getting a shift. Whereas with the girls God only knows where you'll end up. We've ended up in the weirdest of places, and it's all part of the fun of being single. My two friends and I met three lads at a disco one night, and ended up in a flat in Rathmines. There were four lads in the sitting room, all as high as kites, and out of the downstairs toilet appeared a couple dressed up as a priest and a nun. When we saw the set-up we gave each other the 'must get out of here' look and left. Another night we ended up in an all-night drinking pub in Wicklow – the locals were mainly 60-year-old farmers who fell for our charm and bought us drinks all night long. It was great. *Have you ever had a scary experience?* No, touch wood. I think it's all part of the joy of being single. You have to take a risk every now and then, and generally when blokes see that you're just out for the craic they don't expect any more from you.

ROISIN, 25, A WAITRESS FROM LOUTH

Myself and a friend were invited to a party one night. It was totally out of the blue – these two guys approached us in the bar and asked us would we like to go. So we did. Six of us piled into the back of this guy's jeep and headed off. We got to the party, and it was such a seedy place. It was in a stone cottage that had black painted walls and no indoor toilet. All the lads were able to pee outside, but it was a nightmare for the few girls that were present. I headed to the bedroom in search of toilet paper and to my horror I found at least three leather whips, a mirror on the ceiling and porno magazines strewn all over the floor. June and I legged it out of there as fast as we could, and had to walk for at least five miles before we hit the nearest town. We laugh at it now, but I can tell you we were scared shitless then. GERALDINE, 27, A SECRETARY FROM LIMERICK

The late-night or, should I say, 4 a.m. cup of coffee and 'about-last-night' analysis with the girls is the reason why I love being single. Saturday night is our big night out on the town. We have it planned from the previous week, and we know what we're going to wear and where we're going to go. Most of the time, at least one of us will get a shift. We all head back to Maggie's house afterwards and sit around with the fags and the coffee and the all-important Cadbury's Chocolate Fingers! We'll discuss everything from the 'fat cow' who stole the chap that Louise fancied to the 'ride' who ended up on his own. God help whoever got a smooch, 'cause everything, and I mean everything, from the type of kisser he was to the type of jumper he was wearing will be analysed. Of course there's also the nights when someone will be shedding a tear or two, especially if they've overdone it on the drink, and then we all play the Agony Aunt figure to comfort her. But these 'about-last-night' analysis sessions, as we call them, are the best thing about being single. They're better than any man any day! LINDA, 23, AN OFFICE WORKER FROM LEITRIM

I think the more of my friends that 'tie the knot', the more inclined I am not to. I called over to my friend Jenny last week, and was greeted at the door by her snotty-nosed four-year-old son, and a grunt from her husband who had just given her a lecture on why she hadn't his dinner ready on time. My first reaction was to leave all well alone, but I felt she could have done with a bit of support so

I stayed. As I stood at the kitchen sink peeling potatoes I swore that I would never again pray for a boyfriend. I'm not anti-marriage or anti-men, and I know loads of happily married couples, but I'm just not ready for total commitment yet. Men are a novelty for a while, but I can't see myself settling with the one body forever.

MARY, 32, FROM CAVAN

I think people in their late teens and early twenties want to experience a relationship, and for some of them it turns out to be a life of commitment, but for others it just opens the door to a single life. Then, in their late twenties and early thirties, they can either cope with single life or they can't. I'm sure there are thousands of people who are sitting in tonight because they couldn't be bothered facing another uneventful night on the town alone, but it's what you make it. There are some people who are just made for a single life, and others who were made to go down the marriage chute. The reason I'm single is because I choose to be single. I do voluntary work on Saturday mornings with the inner-city kids, and it gives me such satisfaction. When I go out on Saturday nights, I'm out to enjoy myself, not to look for a man. One day, when I decide that I have the time and patience for a man, I'll get one.

LEESA, 25, A BEAUTICIAN FROM DUBLIN

I feel totally content with being single. There is the advantage of independence, being able to get up and just do whatever you want and take off wherever you want to, when you want to. I've got to that stage in my life where I feel an inner contentment. I don't feel the need to have someone to make me complete. I have plenty of male friends, and the biggest disadvantage about being involved with somebody is that you can't talk to and spend time with these lads. I think men are just as possessive as women, and in my experience boyfriends can't cope with a woman having platonic male friends. What really galls me is people going out with people for the sake of it. I personally do not feel the need to stay in a dodgy relationship for fulfilment. I'd prefer to be alone than be with someone who was having a negative effect on my personality.

ANITA, 31, A TEACHER FROM CORK

Conclusion

❝ There's two sides to everything, and I'm not saying that being single is a bed of roses all the time. Sure, there are the good days and the bad days – the days when you fret that maybe you'll never meet someone, and the days when you're glad you haven't met someone. Like anything, it's what you make it. Because of faxes and mobile phones and timed videos and automatic coffee-makers and e-mail, life has become one big 'flight'. Everything is fast and furious. This 'wanted it yesterday' mentality has even seeped into the love and emotional quarter of life. People are craving a successful relationship with a highly intelligent, highly beautiful and extremely wealthy person! What we need to do is take a step back from all of this and slow down. People of the nineties IT [information technology] era need to take stock before it's too late. Relationships are like any other natural human need. Naturally there are people who are extremely content and fulfilled with life and who can survive without a partner, but that need for love and affection will surface one day. When it does, those people who are happy and fulfilled will be lucky enough to have found themselves before they find the 'special other'. But people who are unhappy with single life will never be happy in a relationship.

Relationships don't guarantee happiness. Finding the real you and knowing what really makes you happy is the only solution. Nowadays, people are feeling pressurised into forming a relationship and it has the added pressure of speed – people are jumping in and out of bed with every Tom, Dick and Harry in the search for happiness, and that's wrong. When you are ready to settle with one person and form a lasting relationship it will happen. Love or the pursuit of love was never meant to be a difficult, cruel chore. I think people should do whatever they themselves really want to do. People shouldn't go out with people because they feel it will make Mummy or Daddy happy or because he/she earns a six figure salary. People should just live life as they wish. Being single is not a perfect life, and neither is being married, but it is important to enjoy it – chances are that in the end you'll be either married or single! ❞

Tom, 35, a social worker from Kildare

2. The Downside of Being Single

Galar an grá ná leighiseann luibheanna.
(No herb can cure the pain of love.)

The research suggested that a higher percentage of men than of women are unhappy being single – 46% versus 42%. Among the most commonly given reasons for this unhappiness were loneliness and lack of intimacy, followed closely by the pressure placed on single people by older folk, married friends and relatives. The results of the research appear to tie in with a paper in the *American Journal of Sociology* (reported in *The Sunday Times*, 5 January 1997) which said that 'Men do better out of marriage because women tend to take on more domestic responsibilities as well as a job. Single men are less likely to have someone to care for them and are more likely to live unhealthily.'

Why are women unhappy being single?

❝ I'm so fed up with the 'you'll be left on the shelf', 'you're too fussy', 'why can't you find yourself a nice man and settle down?', 'Ah, sure don't worry, you'll meet him soon' type of comments that we single people have to listen to. Of course it's not easy to be single in a world where having a secure and happy relationship has become a necessary criterion of a happy life. I'm completely aware of the fact that I would have no problem finding a man, but that's just it – I can't find one. So, I have to struggle on without one. I have to endure endless nights of loud rap, funk, punk or whatever they call the music nowadays. I have to explain at least once a week to neighbours, friends, married friends and grannies that, no, I still haven't found a partner. It's a nightmare. It is lonely and saddening that a nice, attractive looking girl like myself can't make it into the successful relationship class. I hate it but I must admit that I'm glad you're doing some research into it. I'd love to know how others survive it.

ROISIN, 30, A TELEPHONIST FROM DUBLIN

It's that sense of not being intimate. The girls are great, but there are things which you wouldn't discuss with girls that you would with a boyfriend. I suppose it's more like your dreams and ambitions. My girlfriends would know what they were, but with a guy it's that sharing of dark secrets and deep dreams about the future and stuff.
PATRICIA, 32, A SECRETARY FROM GALWAY

It's the lack of intimacy. I'd love to have a partner with whom I could share life's little experiences. Going out with the girls gets boring after a while. It's the same old thing. At the start it was enjoyable, but more and more I find myself not bothering to go out.
JOAN, 28, A NURSE FROM LIMERICK

It's getting harder and harder. Discos aren't the way they used to be. I think the nineties have done more harm than good for people. Nowadays, men and women are so caught up with their appearance. It seems like you don't have a chance unless you're wearing a boob tube and have a Kate Moss figure.
JANE, 34, FROM CARLOW, WHO WORKS IN A PHARMACY

The fashion today is tight lycra belly tops and hipsters, which is fine if you have a figure, but for the likes of me it only gets you down. I've no chance dressing the way I do, because fellas would prefer to have a girl with hardly any clothes on as opposed to a 'prude' like me. Being single makes you far too self-conscious and the longer you are alone, the more you get caught up with yourself, which isn't healthy.
JULIE FROM LOUTH

I'd prefer to be going out with someone. There are times in the year when it is almost unbearable – dinner parties, weddings and those dreaded family functions. It's so embarrassing. If you bump into someone that you haven't met in ages, you go through the usual 'how's work?' and then 'how's your love life?' questions. If you're compelled to answer and it's the usual 'I haven't found someone yet' reply, you can almost see in their faces that they are feeling sorry for you. The worst of all was when my friends started having children. I genuinely wasn't interested in listening to their tales of teething and nappy rash. The winter time is especially difficult – there's Christmas, office parties and Valentine's Day. When I was younger it never bothered me 'cause I always thought I'd be married at 30, but now it is tougher. I get depressed about it sometimes and it's hard to pick myself up again. When I go out, I get down because I see all these beautiful young people enjoying themselves and it makes me feel old, and when I stay in I get down 'cause I don't have a boyfriend, so I can't win.   ANNE, 31, A BEAUTICIAN FROM CORK

It gets to the stage where you give up buying sexy lingerie, 'cause there's nobody there to appreciate it. At dinner parties, most people discuss marriage and house prices and I never feel comfortable contributing to the conversation, as I know they think I don't have a clue because I'm single.   FIONA, 29, A RECEPTIONIST FROM ROSCOMMON

The worst thing about being single is not having anybody to go out socialising with, be they male or female. My friends are at different life cycles and are no longer interested in staying out till 4 or 5 a.m. on a Saturday night.   AOIFE, 40, A MIDWIFE FROM DUBLIN

I get paranoid about not having a boyfriend. I start asking myself what is wrong with me that I can't get one. I've tried everything from changing my hairstyle to my clothes, but it doesn't work.
   MANDIE, 23, A SALES ASSISTANT

I miss a regular ration of passion, and unless I'm involved with somebody there is no other way of getting it, as I'm not the type to go out and shark whatever guy comes along.
   IMELDA, 29, A HOTEL MANAGER FROM MAYO

For me, it's simply the feeling of being unloved. You feel like a failure, because you didn't succeed in committing to one man. The late eighties and nineties have seen major changes in Ireland. There's more money and with that goes image – bigger houses, bigger cars, and being in a successful relationship is also a reflection of how well you've done in life. People class you as being 'sad' or 'weird', or think 'there must be something wrong with her' simply because you don't have a partner. It was never easy to be single, and it ain't getting any easier. ANN-MARIE, 33, A SUPERVISOR FROM DUBLIN

I would love to have a boyfriend. I've never had one, and it means I get left out when my friends are discussing theirs. I really would love to meet someone nice. SARAH, 19, A STUDENT FROM CARLOW

It's fun now and then to be single, but I'd prefer to be involved with somebody. There are two things about being single that I'd like to comment on: the fact that it is so annoying when you get the sympathy vote from your friends and family, and the fact that it's very difficult to enjoy yourself when your surrounded by couples on a night out. GRAINNE, 28, A COMPUTER PROGRAMMER FROM LOUTH

I hate being single because I like a regular shift and the attention that you get when you're dating a man. JESSIE, 25, A TEACHER FROM WESTMEATH

I think it's a confidence booster when you have a boyfriend. It's nice to know that there's someone thinking about you and someone to care about you. When you're single you have to fight your own corner, and it's difficult at times. CLODAGH, 25, A FACTORY OPERATIVE FROM TIPPERARY

I miss hearing the words 'I love you'. I haven't had a boyfriend for a year and a half, and I'm not happy as a single soul. I've got so caught up with looking for a boyfriend that I no longer enjoy myself when I go out. I know you're going to tell me that he'll come along when I least expect it and all that lark, but I don't agree. Last January I hardly went out at all, I got very depressed and I'm not ashamed to admit that I even started bingeing on my food. I felt fat and ugly, and no matter what my friends said to the contrary I couldn't see a way out of the vicious black cloud that was hanging over me. I'm a lot better now, but I still get very depressed because of not having a boyfriend. You begin to question everything about yourself and end up super-analysing your looks, your clothes. I even changed my car! It's sad, I know, but that's what being single is like for some people nowadays. SUSAN, 26, A QUALITY CONTROLLER

Approaching 30 was a bit of a disaster. It was a case of 'Oh my God, I've no man'. I was concentrating all my energies on finding a man before I reached 30, but since then, for me anyhow, it has been a lot easier. I have given up on men for the moment, and my career has really taken off. I think it probably has something to do with the fact that I'm not looking any more. Even tonight I was chatted up at the bar – it's great.   AIDEEN, 30, FROM DONEGAL

It's so annoying when you know that your friends and relatives are dying for you to meet someone. If you happen to be doing something different, like going to London for a weekend, your auntie will pop up with 'Oh, that's where you're going to meet him -- that's how Josie met Mick, you know'. And so you head off and despite the fact that you know what your auntie said was rubbish, you still have that sense of 'maybe she's right' in the back of your mind. The boy behind the check-in desk might give you a second glance, and wow, yeah, it all falls into place – it's him!! I know it's sheer childishness, but that's how we women work. I got my fortune told two years ago and she told me I'd end up with a dark-haired man. For at least a year I was totally obsessed and paranoid about every dark-haired man that I met. Never again!   MAURA, 26, A TELESALES CLERK FROM DUBLIN

Because a love life is such a huge part of one's life, it's an even bigger issue when you're single. As you get older you always think that tonight could be the night, so I think people expect too much too soon. You may get lucky and get a shift once in a while, but you'll start planning the rest of your life with this guy after one night with him. I can't remember all the times I've written down my name and his name and done the 'he loves me what %?' on a piece of paper. It's pathetic and childish. I'm 29, and as recently as last week I was doing it. In fact, he's here in the pub tonight, so you never know!
             CLIONA, 29, A STORE MANAGER

Most of my colleagues are married or going out with somebody. On a Monday morning I'd concoct a story about having met someone just to get them interested. The majority of them think I lead a very boring life and that I just sit in and watch videos the whole time.

How wrong they are. I go out most weekends; it's just that I never seem to meet men. They can't understand this, and pity me having to go solo, as they say. It can be very tough, especially in the wintertime when the evenings are dark and you might not feel like getting dressed up to go out. I'd rather sit in and watch a video with a partner, but unfortunately I don't have one.

Kathleen, 32, a social worker

What I detest most about being single is when my friends try to set me up with someone. They'll plan dinner parties around you, and then put you sitting beside a nerd. They'll invite you to parties knowing that you're single, and hope that you will be able to entertain the other single people there. If you are a flirt like my friend is, you'll be number one on the guest list. Will settled people please stop trying to sell us single people off to the first man that their partner wants to see getting 'fixed up'!

Liz, 35, a hairdresser from Fermanagh.

Worse than that is when they automatically assume that you will want to meet this person again. I remember enduring a bore at a dinner party one night out of sheer politeness to my friend, who was the hostess. Looking back, I suppose it did look like I was enjoying his company. There was no opportunity for me to let my single pal know what a bore he actually was. I suffered on, and at the end of the night he asked the hostess's husband for my phone number. She was on cloud nine. 'I'm so happy for you,' she said to me. 'About what?' I asked. 'That Kevin is interested in you – isn't it great?' Needless to say, I sat her down and told her in no uncertain terms that I wasn't the least bit interested.

Liz's friend Karen, 36, a nurse

I think if everybody who's settled and married would just leave us single people alone, we'd be a happier lot. You wonder how they have the time to worry about us in the first place, seeing as how they are supposed to have such a fulfilled and sex-packed married life!

Lassie, 29, from Cork, who is unemployed at the moment

It's the little comments like 'you look nice tonight' or 'you smell nice tonight' that I miss. The girls can tell you till their jaws are sore that you look well, but there's a whole different meaning to it when it comes from a man. I like clothes and keeping myself in shape, and I'd love to have a boyfriend to appreciate it.

PAULA, 27, A BANKER FROM WICKLOW

I'm so fed up with how people treat me simply because I'm single. There are the constant remarks and comments about being 'fussy' and 'hard to please'. I just wish that society would give up its addiction with single people and their life styles.

ÁINE, 39, A SCHOOL PRINCIPAL

Why are men unhappy being single?

Life as a single person is boring. There's much more to do when you have a girlfriend. I hate going to the cinema on my own, and I dread pubs and clubs. I don't drink, so it's even more difficult for me.

SÉAMUS, 25, FROM CORK

I would love to have a girlfriend when I get invited to weddings and parties. No man is an island, and good and all as the lads are, I miss a woman in my life.

DECLAN, 25, A DEPARTMENT OF HEALTH EMPLOYEE FROM KILKENNY

One of the disadvantages of being single is that society sees you as being strange. They think that you must be mean or have a BO problem or something. Most of my customers can't understand why I don't have a girlfriend, and I hate that. They see me as a young, chatty, nice bloke, and all that's missing is a woman. I don't see it like that at all, but because they do, I get a little paranoid and wonder how come I don't have one. I've even pretended to have had a few flings to score a better deal with them, 'cause they get so excited for me.

JAMES, 27, A SALES REP FROM MONAGHAN

I find it very tough being single. My sisters and brothers are all going out with people, and when my sisters ask me for advice on what to buy their boyfriends as presents, I just wish I could have someone nice too.

BRIAN, A MECHANIC FROM LIMERICK

I think it's the anticlimax of not meeting someone that I hate most about being single. I go out with the lads every weekend and we have a laugh and do lads' things, but I'm always hoping that I will meet a girl. But I never do, so I end up going home alone, having to console myself that maybe it'll be next weekend.

PETER, 31, FROM DUBLIN

I simply miss female company. My mother died seven months ago, and I found it very difficult to cope. My friends, both male and female, were all extremely good to me, but I just wanted a big hug from a woman who knew me well. Women have this perception that men are hard-necks, but from where I'm standing, that is not true.

DARREN, 36, A SWIMMING COACH FROM WATERFORD

Having a partner means having a regular sex life, but being single is a curse. You end up in bed alone, and it's cold and unfeeling.

SEÁN. 29, A BUSINESSMAN FROM KERRY

I'm not the type to jump into bed with anyone, but sex is as natural as eating or sleeping and I think it's very important to have a partner to experience it with. I haven't met a girl in two years, which means I've been celibate for that length of time. At the rate I'm going I'd nearly qualify to become a priest! I wouldn't pay for sex; in fact I can't understand how people do. I'll go on hoping that I meet a nice girl soon, but in the meantime I'll have to do with myself.

MICK, 29, A BUS DRIVER FROM OFFALY

I find single life very difficult. It has a huge negative impact on your self-esteem. Most of my friends are happily married with children, and I'm very envious of them. There's only so much you can do on your own. No man is an island, and the world is a lonely place without a special 'other half'. Simple things like going to the cinema are not as enjoyable alone. The first time I went on my own I prayed that I wouldn't bump into any of my students. Even the girl behind the kiosk looked at me with ten heads when I said 'one please', and to make matters worse the only single seat available was in the back row. I felt like running back home, but I survived the ordeal and now I go quite regularly on my own.   GER, 38, A TEACHER FROM DERRY

I've never had a girlfriend, and would love to have one. I don't find shifting different girls all the time very enjoyable. At first it's a bit of a laugh, but after a while the novelty wears off.
                                CONAL, 18, A STUDENT FROM TIPPERARY

You get tired of going out with the lads and doing the same old thing. It gets boring after a while. It would be nice to have a woman to do and share things with. Not just the sex aspect, but buying you presents or being concerned about how well things are going. Lads are lads, and no matter how well you get on with them, there are times when I crave the closeness of a woman.   TONY, 30, A VET FROM LIMERICK

I'm happy and I'm not. Sometimes I wish I could have a girlfriend. I suppose it's wanting the company of a woman. I don't know exactly what it is – all I know is that I miss it. PADRAIG, 28, A FARMER FROM WEXFORD

I love women – their smells, their little hang-ups and all that maternal instinct thing they have. You get sick of going out to have the craic.   MIKE, 23, AN AGRICULTURAL ADVISER FROM GALWAY

I would prefer to be with somebody tonight than be out looking for somebody. It's getting tougher and tougher to find somebody. We're living in a very image-conscious society, and women don't go for genuineness any more. I think they're just out for what they can get and leave. I'd be the first to admit that I don't have film star looks, but I'm no back of a bus either. On more than one occasion, when a woman has found out that I'm a mechanic she's lost interest in me.   TED, 27, A MECHANIC

I would love to have someone to spend my money on. I had a girlfriend for two years, and it was the best time in my life. Stupidly, I fucked up and we ended, but I enjoyed seeing her happy and making her happy. I miss that feeling very much.   MARTIN, 24, A BRICKIE FROM WICKLOW

I feel left out – I suppose it's a bit like a disease. You don't get invited to things because you're single. Women get accused of being obsessed with their biological clock, but from a male point of view there's the whole issue of having children also. I'd love to have a wife and children one day, and it is very upsetting at times to think that I may never have that. People automatically think that men can cope with singledom, but I find it very difficult. I'd even go as far as saying that it can be depressing at times.

Pat, 42, a scientist from Tyrone

I feel the pain of being single especially in the winter time. I know all my mother's Christmases would come at once if I found a woman. There's a type of enjoyment that comes with a heterosexual relationship that you could never get from your mates.

Victor, 29, a farmer from Kerry

I find it very hard. All my mates, without exception, are going out with people so they're never in the mood to head to a night club after the pub. Hence I end up going home alone.

Derek, 28, who works in a computer factory

I miss the 'one on one' that you get when you're seeing a girl. I like girls and find most of them very interesting and enjoy their company. I miss that the most.

Seán, 24, a carpenter from Galway

I'm a nicer person when I have a girlfriend. I don't know whether it's their hormones or what that calm me down, but I am a lot nicer to live with when I'm involved in a relationship.

Joe, 30, a sales rep from Dublin

Even amongst the lads, I get slagged off for not having a girlfriend. Most of the time it's just a joke about having smelly feet or farting, but yeah, I do get slagged off. My granny on my father's side loves me to bits and is always saying that I'm better off without a woman, but then I can't take her to bed with me on a Friday night!

Jason, 33, a pharmacist from Waterford

I hate the innuendoes about being single. Most of the lads have girlfriends, and that's fine with me. They're always there when I need them, and we all have a serious 'studs only' session once a month. But I do often wonder what it would be like to be going out with someone. I work in the family butchers' and I have often overheard my ma asking the customers whether their daughters would be keen on me. It used to upset me, but I've learned to laugh it off now. But I do get the 'is this it, will we finally be getting a day out?' remarks also.
Tom, 28, a butcher from Kilkenny

Conclusion

I was astounded to meet such a huge number of genuinely nice, attractive men and women who are unhappy being single. I noticed that those individuals who are happy being single have taken time to create a social life outside the typical social scene. I'd be the first to admit that the pub and club scene becomes boring and disheartening, but I have learned that being happy regardless of whether you are single or in a relationship is what is important. Maybe society is too concerned with image – maybe everybody is so caught up with trying to find happiness that we are losing out in the pursuit of it. It is far healthier to be happy with oneself first, and then the person for you will come along. As Tom, the social worker from Kildare, said at the end of Chapter 1 – 'Relationships don't guarantee happiness. Finding the real you and knowing what really makes you happy is the only solution.' Then and only then will you be in the right frame of mind to seek a partner.

Regarding the pressure from older folk to get hitched, I learned myself from the Singles Ball that when you do get too caught up with trying to find a partner, you'll never find one. It's only a topic of conversation for those older people. Think about it – how often have you asked a recently married couple how's married life treating them? It's the same thing.

Confidence is about how high your level of self-esteem is. When we realise what we have to offer and firmly believe in ourselves, our self-esteem level rises and we give off a confident aura. Of course, a spate of rejection and a 'famine', as one interviewee put it, can shatter your confidence. Because we can't see exactly how other people see us, it is difficult to judge whether we are attractive or not. Remember, 'sometimes all that's needed to be attractive is a smile', as Pamela, a 30-year-old air hostess from Dublin, said. However, one thing is for sure – we can all spot a desperate man or woman a mile away. The 'eau de desperation', as Stephen, a friend of mine, calls it, is a sure way to turn somebody off you.

In the end, I think it is important that we don't end up like Patrick Kavanagh, who spent all his life waiting on his mother to die so that he could move a woman into the house. His mother lived a lot longer than he thought she would, and one day he stood at the front door asking the question – 'Did life ever happen?'

 What Do Women Look For in a Man?

Ní hí an áilleacht a chuireann an corcán ag fiuchaidh.
(Beauty doesn't boil the pot.)

How many times have you looked in the mirror and thought 'Will he/she like me in this?', 'Is my bum sticking out?', 'Have I overdone it on the aftershave?', 'Does the shirt go with the trousers?', 'Is my hair OK?', etc., etc. Let's face it – the mating game is a marketing game.

Just like products on a supermarket shelf that are packaged attractively, we humans subconsciously 'package' ourselves in the most attractive way possible. Or at least we think we're packaged attractively. But what do women really look for in a man? Is it looks, personality, wealth or a sense of humour?

The female interviewees were asked what attracted them to the opposite sex. They were also asked for comments about 'pet hates' and favourite outfits on men.

25% of the 439 girls said that insincerity was their biggest pet hate in regard to men. A good personality is the most sought-after quality. In relation to appearance and dress – men, if you don't have a pair of chinos and a chunky sweater, go out and buy them fast!

Most girls agreed that first impressions are very important, but if a man has a lousy personality, then it won't work. 'Sometimes,' as Doreen, a 29-year-old from Limerick, said, 'you may be attracted to a man because you know him even though he may not necessarily possess the qualities that you would look for on a 'first impressions' basis.'

What attracts you to the opposite sex?

❝ Honesty and a good personality. Looks are important to a certain extent, but what's the point in having a George Clooney on your arm when he has a personality like a dishcloth?

ANGELA, 28, A PRODUCTION WORKER

Sincerity – I like lads to be sincere. I can't stand posers and bull-shitters. Unfortunately, there aren't too many sincere ones around. The posers and bullshitters are two a penny. You know the types – the ones you can hear before you even get to the pub. They'll brag about how much they earn or what they drive – puke.

LEESA, 25, A BANK OFFICIAL FROM DUBLIN

Looks. Initially, I'll be attracted to looks and then personality. I think you need to have both to be able to go out with somebody. Looks are fine for a one-night stand but for the longer term it's essential that they have a good personality.

KATHY, 28, A SECONDARY TEACHER FROM LAOIS

Looks are and always will be a huge part of the attractiveness of a man. But looks can be over-rated. Invariably, the best-looking guys are dickheads. For a relationship to develop, you need to be able to get on well together. COLETTE, 28, AN OPTICIAN FROM DOWN

As you get older, you learn that all the qualities you would have hoped to find in a man dwindle. Or you may find that your obsession with rich men has disappeared. With age you learn what the important qualities are. It's not a case of settling for second best; it's simply the fact that you realise that it takes more than looks to make a relationship work. KATHERINE, 34, A CIVIL SERVANT FROM MONAGHAN

Men. Simply and plainly men. My nickname is 'nymphomaniac', and I didn't get that for nothing. I just adore men, everything about them. ORLA, 23, A PRODUCTION WORKER FROM DUBLIN

I think looks are very important. I don't care how tall or small he is, but he has to be good-looking. Body-wise, he'd have to have a firm bum. As far as I'm concerned, if he doesn't have a bum he has nothing. SHAUNA, 28, AN ACCOUNTING TECHNICIAN FROM WATERFORD

Aftershave – it drives me wild. I'm an expert on aftershaves and can tell a good one from a bad one in a second. For me, it's very important for a man to smell nice. Years ago in Ireland it would have been unheard of for a man to wear aftershave or, God forbid, moisturiser. And I hate people who say that the only men who wear moisturiser are gay. That's not the case – it's important for men to take care of their appearance, and for me the smell of aftershave is plain sexy. He may not look like anything, but at least he'll smell like something.   DEIRDRE, 29, A CLERK FROM KILKENNY

Nice hands. I hate a man with wimpy hands – I like big broad hands, and it's nothing to do with the size of a man's hands reflecting the size of certain organs. I'm just attracted to nice big hands.
CELINE, 33, AN ESTATE AGENT

Honesty – plain old-fashioned honesty. I think it's the most important factor regarding the opposite sex. If he's not honest, you haven't a hope in hell of having a successful relationship. I also like a sporty type of man; they're fit, well toned and great in bed.
ANNE, 24, A TRAINEE ACCOUNTANT FROM MAYO

Men who work with their hands are very sexy – builders, carpenters, painters. I was driving home one day and I saw this guy hitching; he was in a pair of paint-splashed overalls with a rucksack thrown over his shoulder, and I had to fight the urge to get him into the car and have my wicked way with him!
EMMA, 21, A POSTWOMAN FROM KILDARE

Shoes. I always look at a man's shoes. I like them to be wearing a nice pair of shoes. I know this may sound a bit clichéd, but black shoes and white socks are just a big no-no. As for grey shoes, good God, how did they ever find a place on the shop shelves? How can men in the whole of their senses buy them, let alone wear them – they're repulsive!   RUTH, 34, AN ACCOUNTANT FROM KERRY

I need a man to be a man. My biggest pet hate is one of these 'new men' types who does all the women's work and helps around the house and stuff. Forget it – I'll do the crying myself, thanks very much. And eyes are important too – I love men with nice eyes. Eyes can tell so much about a person. There's nothing more annoying than a man who doesn't talk into your eyes.   ANNE, 27, A FARMER FROM WICKLOW

Money. I love wealthy men. Wealth, as Zsa Zsa Gabor said, is the biggest aphrodisiac of all. It's great when you're dating a man with loads of money, 'cause he'll have a nice car, a nice house and buy you lovely gifts.

SHARON, 25, FROM DUBLIN

Spectacles. I adore men who wear glasses. I bet that's the first time you got that as a reply! I think it makes them look sexy and intelligent. Most of my friends hate guys who wear glasses, but I love them. Maybe it's got something to do with my Dad wearing them – I don't know.

GERALDINE, 27, A SECRETARY FROM LIMERICK

Flat stomachs. Men go on about women's stomachs, yet they never think that we may not be attracted to their beer bellies. A bit of a stomach is fine, but I can't abide lads who have big flabby beer bellies that hit off their toes. It's repulsive.

ALISON, 23, A FITNESS INSTRUCTOR FROM WESTMEATH

I love a man who has a nice body. There's nothing more attractive than a well-toned torso on a man. It's a real turn-on for me.

LORRAINE, 23, AN ARTIST

For me it's a complete turn-off when a man has four or five bellies. Leaving out the problem of getting squashed to bits, I find it disgusting. I think overweight men are worse than overweight women. I can't help thinking that they're of the 'couch potato' type – lazy, basically.

MAGGIE, 24, FROM LEITRIM, WHO WORKS FOR A FOOD COMPANY

I love a man to have a bit of 'get up and go'. It's so much more interesting if a guy has an interesting life outside the hours of 9 to 5. I'd much rather a man who had a hobby. Whatever about girls being addicted to *Coronation Street*, to me it's a massive negative if he can't see me because he has to watch Vera Duckworth!

CAROLINE, A PUBLIC RELATIONS EXECUTIVE FROM DUBLIN

I fall for accents in a big way. Northern ones are especially sexy, not to mention French men speaking broken English. Oh my God, it's just such a turn-on!

PAULA, 27, A BANKER

I'm attracted to accents. Even Southern accents are cute, but first on my list would have to be foreign men's accents. I also have a weak spot for husky voices. You know, the ones that send shivers down your spine. I love them.
MADGE, 33, A TEACHER FROM MEATH

He'd have to be good in bed. I've done my ABCs in lovemaking, and I certainly don't want to go through it again. Basically what I'm looking for is a man with plenty of sexual experience.
JENNY, 39, AN OFFICE WORKER

Judging by the boys I've gone out with, I'd have to say I'm attracted to the 'baddies'. There's just something so desirable about them – I like the challenge in them.
HELEN, 33, A CLERK FROM CORK

I always go for the dickheads – I know they'll treat me like shit, but I do it every time. I'm tired hearing my friends say 'hope you've learned your lesson now', but I never do. Why?
AISHLING, 21, A WAITRESS FROM KERRY

Legs and bums. I adore men with long legs. I remember seeing this guy in a video shop one day, and he was just standing there sifting through the videos. Well, he had the longest pair of legs I've ever seen and was wearing blue Lee corduroys. I nearly had an orgasm on the spot! Bums are very important also.
LIZANNE, 34, A TEACHER FROM DONEGAL

Lips. Big motherfucker ones like Mike Tyson or George Clooney. They're so amazing. I wouldn't care if he was a weed as long as he had big lips.
SHAUNA, 22, FROM KILDARE

Generosity. And I don't want you thinking I'm into men for what I can get out of them. Not that at all. Very simply, I like a chap who won't mind buying a drink for me or my friends every now and then. Actually, I broke it off with a boyfriend because of it. He was mean.
CIARA, 22, WHO WORKS IN A CLOTHES STORE

'Sense of humour' was a very common reply – almost 28% of girls are attracted to men with a sense of humour.

> I think a sense of humour is the most important thing. Looks are important to a certain degree, but it's great to be in the company of a man who can make you laugh.
> SARAH, 32, A NURSE FROM LIMERICK

> Sense of humour, a nice guy, not a bullshitter. I like a decent type of man. A lot of fellas are just out for the craic at the end of the day, and you don't trust them.
> MICHELLE, 31, A MIDWIFE FROM GALWAY

> Sense of humour is very important. A lot of lads are just boring. They may have fabulous looks and a great body, but for me it's a complete turn-off if they aren't able to relax and have the craic.
> TRACEY, 21, A SHOP ASSISTANT FROM LONGFORD

31% of the women interviewed were attracted to 'a good personality' – I asked a few of them what exactly they meant by this.

> Someone you can have the craic with and also be able to talk to. An interesting person. I mean someone you can get along with on a serious level and out socially. Definitely not someone who won't listen to you and is always talking about themselves.
> MARY, A 'COMPUTER FREAK'

> Personality is everything, from how they treat you to how they behave in public. Basically, a good personality is someone who is not boring, self-consumed or mean.
> MAGGIE, 24, FROM LEITRIM, WHO WORKS FOR A FOOD COMPANY

> Personality for me is the 'make-up' of an individual. Boring men, for example, don't make for good personalities.
> SINÉAD, 24, FROM ROSCOMMON

> I suppose it's a combination of having a good sense of humour, a bit of general cop-on and being attentive to a woman's needs.
> SARAH, 32, A NURSE FROM LIMERICK

What are your pet hates in men?

My biggest pet hate would have to be men who can't handle their drink. It's such a turn-off.
ROISIN, 25, A WAITRESS FROM LOUTH

My number one pet hate would have to be a 'walk-over' of a man.
HELEN, 33, A CLERK FROM CORK

I hate men who are possessive. It's like they want to control everything you do and say and interrogate you when you've been apart. To me, it's a sign of insecurity, and a possessive man is someone I'd steer well clear of.
FIONA, 32, A TEACHER FROM TYRONE

Big turn-offs for me are posers and braggers. Posers are those types that think they're God's gift to creation. They'll drive flashy cars and bore you to tears with how good they find the £1,000 a year gym. Braggers are those types who boast about everything. Honestly, it wouldn't surprise me if they brag about having regular bowel movements. They're bores and should carry a label saying 'DO NOT TOUCH – EXPLOSIVE', 'cause when they start talking they'll never stop!
FIONA, 30, A BANKER FROM DUBLIN

My big pet hate is men who brag about how much they drink – 'I drank ten pints and six shorts and was still able to walk in a straight line' crap. They'll line up along the bar and knock the beer into them as if it was going out of fashion. It's disgusting. Then they'll fall around the place belching and farting and rub up against any passing women and make crude comments.
NICOLA, 24, FROM GALWAY

Meanness – I hate a mean lad. Fine if he's unemployed or a student, but those Scrooge types are a complete no-no, and I'm not just talking about money. It includes being mean with their compliments and emotional support. What is the point in having a boyfriend who won't listen to your problems and give you advice etc.? Basically, to be there for you when you need him.
MAURA, 26, A TELESALES CLERK FROM DUBLIN

I think men are under the impression that women are out to get what they can out of them, but I personally don't know any girl who is like that. I think it's in our nature to be generous, and we give without expecting anything in return. Of course there are plenty of girls out there 'using' men and giving the rest of us a bad name. But I sincerely think that most girls enjoy having a man buy them a drink every now and then. Don't the lads get repaid in other ways?

SIOBHAN, 29, A DRESSMAKER

A scabby man would definitely rate very low in my book. I don't expect men to pay for everything, but it's nice when a man buys you a drink. You'll end up buying the second drink and carry on from there, so it's even in the end. But I cannot handle mean men.

ÁINE, 39, A SCHOOL PRINCIPAL

My biggest pet hate is men who wear their jeans just sitting across their arses. When they raise up or bend down you can see the cracks of the white cheeks – it's revolting.

LIZANNE, 34, A TEACHER FROM DONEGAL

Men who automatically assume that you'll ride them. I was in a pub one time and this guy walked up to me and said 'if I wasn't knocking off my girlfriend, I'd be knocking you off'. It was disgusting, and I wouldn't mind but if he'd been the last guy on the planet I wouldn't have gone near him.

GER, 26, FROM DERRY

Men who go on and on about their ex-girlfriends – it's a complete turn-off.

NOREEN, A PERSONAL ASSISTANT FROM TIPPERARY

Men who don't understand women. It's so annoying. OK, we have active hormones, but so do they – it's just that women like to discuss things and analyse things. Men can't understand that at all. I think it's only natural to have hang-ups about our bodies and our looks; where's the harm in talking about it? But most men just don't want to listen.   PAULINE, 23, FROM SLIGO, WHO WORKS IN A GARDEN CENTRE

Nose-picking was a very common 'pet hate'.

> It's vulgar and disgusting. And I don't care what people say to the contrary, but most men pick their noses in the car when stuck at traffic lights – in fact I'd go as far as saying that all men have, at some stage, picked their nose in public. PATRICIA, 32, A SECRETARY FROM GALWAY

> Picking their noses is not so bad, but when they roll it around between their fingers, that's what sickens me. I'd love to know if they have competitions amongst themselves as to who can find the biggest one! It's repulsive. MAUREEN, 28, A PE TEACHER FROM CORK

> Speaking as a blonde, I'd have to say that one of the most annoying things about men is that they assume all blondes are bimbos. Numerous guys have looked at me with ten heads when I told them that I was a teacher. To make matters worse, they'd reply in shock 'Oh – a primary school teacher?' It really sickens me. LIZ, 33, A SECONDARY TEACHER FROM KILDARE

'Two-timing' was also a popular 'pet hate'.

> What I'd love to know is why do they do it? It is so unfair. As they get older the majority of them cop on, but young lads are the worst for it. BETTY, 23, FROM DUBLIN

> It is so unfair – they risk everything for the sake of somebody else's saliva. I can't understand it. DOLORES, 24, A NANNY FROM MEATH

> Hairy backs would be a big pet hate of mine. Sometimes you meet a really nice bloke and then see the hair through his shirt – yuk. ROISIN, 30, A TELEPHONIST FROM DUBLIN

> Track suits. They don't suit any man – even the men on the fitness videos look hideous in them. I wish men would learn that we girls hate them. Aside from the fact that all their wobbly bits are hanging loose, they make them look like a pair of tights that's been filled with potatoes. TANYA, 34, A SELF-EMPLOYED GRAPHIC ARTIST

> I must admit that I find good-looking men intimidating. I'd steer clear of them at all costs. They're too caught up with how they look, and that frightens me, I guess. LORNA, 26, A BARPERSON FROM CLARE

Beards – I hate them. I think they're dirty. What attracts me is a clean-cut man, nicely dressed, clean fingernails and hair that's not overgrown or in need of a clippers. I hate a man who doesn't have an interest in his appearance. It automatically means that he'd have very little, maybe no, interest in you either.

Sarah, 23, a student from Galway

BO. In this day and age, it's completely unacceptable for anybody to have a body odour problem.   Colette, 28, an optician from Down

Smoking is a big turn-off for me. I hate smoke, and it's often happened that I meet a nice lad but as soon as I discover he smokes I lose all interest immediately.   Sile, 24, who works in a crèche

What's your favourite outfit on a man?

Chunky sweaters. There's nothing nicer than a man who wears chunky sweaters and desert boots. I hate men who always wear a shirt and tie.   Mary, 36, a receptionist from Dublin

I can't stand it when a man is always wearing a shirt and tie – it's as if he's bringing his work with him everywhere he goes and that he can't relax.   Claire, 38, a legal secretary from Louth

I love casual clothes on a man – chinos and a casual shirt. I'm not into labels, and I hate the rugby shirt types who wear their collars standing up. That's a real turn-off for me.

Jane, 25, a sales assistant from Limerick

Casual jeans and shirts – not leather jackets.

Tracey, 21, a shop assistant from Longford

Monkey suits – there is something so attractive about a man in a monkey suit.   Noreen, a personal assistant from Tipperary

Most guys look better in a suit, and it's nice for special occasions, but not within 25 yards of a pub, thanks very much. Casual jeans and shirts for socialising.   Mary, a 'computer freak'

Women's top ten 'pet hates' regarding men

1. Insincerity/sarcasm.
2. Posing/excessive concern with their looks.
3. Meanness.
4. Not taking an interest in their appearance.
5. Drink too much/bragging about how much they drink.
6. Hairy backs.
7. Constantly 'eyeing up' other women in their girlfriends' company.
8. Picking their noses, spitting and cursing.
9. Complaining.
10. Laziness/lack of 'get up and go'.

Top five qualities women seek in a man

1. Good personality.
2. Sense of humour.
3. Sincerity, genuineness, honesty.
4. Understanding of women.
5. Good looks.

Most common comments regarding men's clothes

1. Like chunky sweaters and jeans.
2. Like casual clothes and chinos.
3. Dislike track suits, leather jackets and black and grey shoes with white socks.
4. Dislike 'jeans hanging around their arses'.
5. Like good shoes.

Most popular physical features of a man

1. Eyes.
2. Bums.
3. Legs.
4. A smile.
5. Hands.

Most common pet hates regarding appearance, etc.

1. Body odour.
2. Beards.
3. Brown teeth.
4. Drunkenness.
5. Dirty fingernails.

4 What Do Men Look For in a Woman?

Ní dhéanfaidh an saol capall rása d'asal.
(You can't make a racing horse from a donkey.)

Most women spend a fortune on their appearance, hair styles, make-up, clothes – some even spend £50 or £60 getting the 'colour me beautiful' done. Of course some females do all this for themselves, and not for the opposite sex as men would like to believe. Most girls will agree that having a shower and putting on a bit of make-up is done purely to make them feel good about themselves. However, at the weekend it's a different ball game – you're out to impress. If it's a special date or a special party where the person you're after is going to be, you'll start planning the outfit weeks in advance. Who can honestly deny having pulled out and tried on at least five different outfits in one night? It's all part of the fun, but at the time it's a nightmare. Your friend likes the red shirt, you prefer the blue one; your brother tells you that your bum is sticking out, your sister thinks you should put your hair up, your friend likes it down, your father thinks you look like a tart. God, it's pure hell!

The male interviewees were asked what attracted them to the opposite sex. They were also asked for comments about 'pet hates' and favourite outfits on women.

The results shocked me. I know now why I'm single at 29! I would tend to be too flirtatious and independent, which is a huge turn-off, apparently. Plus about a million other things that I do.

What I found interesting about what men find attractive in a woman is that good looks are the most sought-after feature, with personality in second place, whereas with the women personality was number one and good looks were ranked number five. Does this tell us something about how different the sexes really are?

What attracts you to the opposite sex?

 Sex.   Stephen, 33, a shop owner from Dublin

Eyes. They are a huge turn-on for me. And I especially love it when a girl smiles with her eyes.   James, 27, a sales rep from Monaghan

Looks – I definitely like a good-looking girl. I'd be a liar if I said otherwise. I'm not into Barbie Doll types 'cause they are bimbos. Simply, attractive looking girls.   Tony, 30, a vet from Limerick

A girl you can have a laugh with.   Derek, 27, a carpenter from Carlow

Legs like the Eiffel Tower, slim on bottom and broad child-bearing hips on top.   Stephen, 39, a truck driver from Cavan

Good try, Stephen, but the Eiffel Tower is the other way round!

She'd have to have good legs or I wouldn't even give her a second glance. I also have a soft spot for continental women.
    Tom, 24, an army officer from Kildare

Intelligence. I love an intelligent woman – not necessarily a PhD head, simply a woman with a brain. Nothing worse than a girl who can only talk about her nails, her hair or her spots! I also like women with a nice laugh – I hate those hyena laughers. I don't know how anybody can put up with them. As for clothes, I love a woman in a pair of Levi's 501s – KISS (keep it simple, stupid). Simple and plain, jeans and a clean blouse.
    Joe, 28, an auctioneer from Tipperary

Tits.   John Paul, 18, a student from Cork

The fact that they are opposite, and opposites attract.
    Ciaran, 21, who's unemployed at the moment

I like natural women and women who are themselves. Make-up is a huge turn-off for me. Do women look at themselves in the mirror

before they leave the house? They have orange faces and then a big white neck – it's pantomine material, not something for the hunting game.
Paul, 35, a factory operative from Donegal

Nice dressers – I love a woman who can dress well. Not women who wear skirts up to their fannies.
Stewart, 35, a businessman from Cork

Personality is very important – if she doesn't have a personality, you can forget it.
Cormac, 20, a student from Laois

I like a bit of meat – there is nothing nicer than a few love handles. It is a thousand times more attractive than a girl who's only a bag of bones. You might as well be riding a bicycle.
Martin, a plumber from Sligo

Girls you can have the craic with. Plain and simple, a girl who can make me laugh. You need a woman who can get along with you and your mates. They have to be able to enjoy the craic and not be too caught up with how they look or what car you drive.
Andrew, 23, an electrician from Louth

Red hair and freckles – maybe because it's so rare. Have you met any on your travels? Last summer I met the nicest girl in the world and she had red hair and freckles, and I'll never go back to blondes again. She was delicious! Of course personality is very important. More and more women are so caught up with themselves that they can't relax and enjoy life, and that's a big turn-off for me.
Declan, 25, who works for the Department of Health

I like a woman to be a woman. They were born to be feminine and there is nothing more attractive than a woman who's not afraid to be a woman. To care and show concern and be motherly is what I'm after in a woman.
Donal, 23, a builder from Kildare

I think that nowadays too many girls have gone overboard with the whole feminist thing. The opposite sex don't know what they want. In the end, they won't be the ones in the winning enclosure 'cause we'll give up buying them dinner and sending them flowers.
A 25-year-old jockey from Meath

I've got to say that I am attracted to real women – women who are aware of the power they can have over a man, i.e. their natural female aura. I suppose there is a lot of truth in the 'Irish mother' theory – in the past Irish men were mollycoddled by their mothers, so they will expect the same treatment from their wives and girlfriends. There is this weird mother and son bond, and subconsciously we are looking for our mother in the women we meet. I'm not criticising Irish mothers, but I don't think that Irish women of the nineties want to treat men the way their mothers did.

BRIAN, 26, A BANK OFFICIAL FROM TIPPERARY

Girls who are very good looking.   JIMMY, 19, A STUDENT FROM GALWAY

Uniforms. I love women in uniforms, especially those white see-through ones where you get a look at their knickers. They're A-OK, man. My pet hate is frilly dresses that go to the ankles.

SÉAN, 25, A SALES REP FROM CORK

In relation to physique, boobs are number one, followed by bums and eyes. You can't beat a woman with a bit of cushioning on the behind. It makes the ride all the more smooth!

VICTOR, 29, A FARMER FROM KERRY

Tits. I love women's tits. Size is not important. My pet hate is smoking – it just doesn't suit girls. Unfortunately, more and more girls are smoking nowadays. It's a filthy habit.

TONY, A MECHANIC FROM WATERFORD

What are your pet hates in women?

I cannot handle nags. They, to me are the saddest bunch of people in society. Everything from the weather, to the pub being packed is a cause for complaint with them – yuk.

DEREK, 27, A CARPENTER FROM CARLOW

A big turn-off for me is women who wear short skirts and no tights. It's revolting. Go down any Irish street in the middle of the fabulous summers that we get and I can guarantee you that you'll see women in shorts or skirts with big white flabby legs – wicked altogether.

Tom, 24, an army officer from Kildare

Indecision, that's what drives me mad about girls. They never know where they want to go, and when I decide to go somewhere they'll have a face as long as O'Connell Street for the rest of the day 'cause I made the decision. When a girl says 'I don't mind', it means 'I mind a lot'.

Con, 24, from Dublin

Loud mouths, the types that should have been born with a penis. They shout, take control of the conversation and then scream – horrible.

Paudie, 26, from Cork

Handbags are a big pet hate of mine. Why do so many girls carry handbags? In the name of God, what do they be carrying in them?

Conor, 32, a general operative

Easy women. I was in a Dublin hotel one Friday night and there was this tall blonde babe standing at the bar, so I decided, for the hell of it, to ask her out to dance. Well I'm not joking you, we were all of about 10 seconds on the floor when she opened her mouth. That was it, I can tell you, it was such a turn-off.

Liam, 32, a marketing executive from Kildare

Ski pants. You can see all their bits and pieces and it doesn't matter what size they are – fat or skinny – they are horrible.

Gerry, a farmer from Laois

Ski pants. I absolutely hate them. They don't suit any girl. Why do ye wear them? It's as good as if men went around in tights.

Simon, a freelance journalist from Dublin

Women drivers. I've just come from the races and, no joke, this girl stalled the whole lane of traffic because she was in the wrong lane. it must be true that a short skirt will get you anything – even your driving test.

Frank, 30, a doctor from Galway

Tracksuits and stilettos or ski pants and stilettos – vile.

GEORGE, 45, A TAXI DRIVER FROM DUBLIN

Those earrings they wear in their noses.

PAT, A FARMER FROM MAYO WHO WOULDN'T REVEAL HIS AGE

Dyed blonde hair with black roots. It's cheap and common. I don't know why so many women dye their hair blonde. Take a look at the Spanish women, who are the best looking women in the world, in my view, and they never dye their hair blonde. Natural colours are best.

SÉAMUS, A POSTMAN FROM DUBLIN

There's a huge myth surrounding blonde hair. Me or me mates wouldn't go out of our way to meet a blonde. Back in the sixties, the Marilyn Monroe thing probably had a lot to do with the 'blondes are more fun' image. Real blondes or nothing, in my book.

JOHN, 23, A STUDENT FROM LIMERICK

Drunk women. I know this is a purely sexist comment, but drunk men are bearable but drunk women – forget it. Last year I saw this girl totally plastered on the floor in my local rugby club, and none of her friends were to be seen. It was saddening.

PAT, 25, FROM WICKLOW

I think people associate drunk women with cheapness and the fact that lads will take advantage of them in a vulnerable state. I've often heard the lads say that they love it when their girlfriends are drunk 'cause they'd do anything for them. At the end of the day, women have far more to lose by getting drunk than men have. I'd also like to say that women who flash too much are a big pet hate of mine. A mini skirt is fine, but not one that goes way up. Boobs as well – I think too many women wear clothes that are far too revealing. It's great on someone else's girlfriend, but not on my girlfriend.

DERMOT, 34, FROM DUBLIN

Women complaining about their weight and being obsessed with dieting.

BRENDAN, A GOLF PROFESSIONAL

It appears to be far more acceptable in the country than in the bigger towns and cities for women to drink pints. As one guy put it – 'If my girlfriend was meeting my parents for the first time, they wouldn't be at all impressed if she ordered a pint.'

There is nothing more annoying than when you take a girl out to dinner and she just sits there picking at her food. Needless to say, they very rarely have a dessert – it annoys the crap out of me.
JOE, 37, A FACTORY MANAGER FROM DUBLIN

Fine if they are on a diet and need to be on one, but too many women are caught up with their weight. I don't know where women ever got the notion that men like skinny girls, because we genuinely don't. Skin and bone is only fit for the dog. A skinny girl is a big pet hate of mine.
CATHAL, 35, A BANK OFFICIAL FROM LOUTH

Smoking. Girls who smoke and curse are my two pet hates.
MURT, 33, A FITNESS INSTRUCTOR AND PART-TIME BOUNCER FROM DONEGAL

Women who smoke on the street. I can't wait till it's banned.
MIKE, 26, A QUANTITY SURVEYOR FROM WEXFORD

Nags are my pet hate. Whatever about having to answer to your boss, but having to explain to a woman where you've been and with whom and how many pints you had is a joke.
SCOTT, 24, A SOLICITOR FROM DUBLIN

One of the most common complaints was the inability of women to understand men.

Seriously, I've given up on the female race – they are so confused and confusing. You cannot win, regardless of what you do. They'll give you a night out with the lads and tell you to enjoy yourself, so you go out, and five hours later with eight or nine pints on you, you might decide to phone them 'cause you're feeling horny. But they'll scream down the phone at you – 'Who was she?'. They automatically think that you have shifted somebody else and are ringing to apologise. If you don't ring you'll be accused of all sorts of misdemeanours. It's an ordeal. They don't know what they want, so how the hell are we supposed to know?

RON, 38, A LORRY DRIVER FROM DUBLIN

Men and women are so completely different, if you ask me – we are just not as emotional as they are. Plus, we aren't able to say things like 'I love you' with any ease. With a few drinks any old fool will slur out the words 'I love you', but in a sober frame of mind it is a very hard thing to say. Women don't understand men, and that's a fact of life.

TIMMY, 26, A FARMER FROM SLIGO

I think too many women think all men are bastards, so they tar us all with the same brush. They automatically think that if you pass a comment about a girl, you just want to get into her knickers. They'll never understand the concept of bonding with the lads and enjoying a few beers with them. PAT, 36, FROM CLARE, WHO IS SELF-EMPLOYED

Why do so many girls play hard to get? I always thought they were supposed to be the ones who could handle their emotions and be able to lay the cards on the table, but I've yet to come across a girl who is up front. They'll tease the jocks off you and then coolly leave with 'See ya now'.

JIM, 22, FROM OFFALY

A high proportion of men hate girls who talk about their old boyfriends.

It's so annoying when girls go on about their ex-boyfriends. To me it's a real sign of insecurity. CHRIS, 32, AN ENGINEER FROM TIPPERARY

It's as good as saying 'I don't really want to be with you; I'd prefer to be with him'. I always finish it with a girl who moans on about exs.

PADDY, 36, A GOVERNMENT WORKER FROM CLARE

I hate it – it's a real insecurity thing. I'm a man and I wouldn't listen to that kind of bullshit. It reminds me of me ma when I was younger, the way she compared me to me brothers and friends – 'Why can't you do your homework or tidy your room like they do?', so being human I do the opposite. I give girls the boot if they carry on about old flames. BARRY, A CONSTRUCTION WORKER FROM MEATH

What's your favourite outfit on a woman?

❝ Her birthday suit.   JOE, 37, A FACTORY MANAGER FROM DUBLIN

Leather gear is a big turn-on for me, especially if they have the figure for it.   CONOR, 32, A GENERAL OPERATIVE

Skirts – it's not fashionable for girls to wear skirts out socially any more, and that's a shame as most girls have great legs and they are no good to any man hidden under a pair of trousers.
                         BEN, FROM CORK, WHO WORKS IN ELECTRONICS

I like a woman to wear classy clothes, not cheap hipsters or belly tops.   JIM, 22, FROM OFFALY

Belly tops and rings in their bellies are a real hit with me.
                         TONY, 21, A MECHANIC FROM WATERFORD

Men's top ten 'pet hates' regarding women

1. Drunkenness.
2. Nagging – girls who complain and moan the whole time.
3. Posing/snobbiness – girls who think no man is good enough for them.
4. Bossiness/domineering women.
5. Cursing.
6. Smoking.
7. Ski pants.
8. Playing hard to get.
9. Women drivers.
10. Picky eaters.

Top five qualities men seek in a woman

1. Good looks.
2. Good personality.
3. Sense of humour.
4. Ability to understand men.
5. To be easy-going and 'out for the craic'; not to moan.

Most common comments regarding women's clothes

1. More girls should wear skirts.
2. Leather trousers and skirts are very sexy.
3. Ski pants are a huge turn-off.
4. Men dislike very low-cut tops and 'flashing too much flesh at every man in the place'.
5. Stilettos should be thrown out.

Most popular physical features of a woman

1. Eyes.
2. Boobs.
3. Legs.
4. Buttocks.
5. A good body – not skinny.

Most common pet hates regarding appearance etc.

1. Too much make-up.
2. Drunkenness.
3. Dyed blonde hair with dark roots.
4. Hairy armpits.
5. Being overweight.

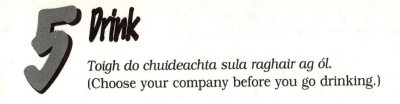

5 Drink

Toigh do chuideachta sula raghair ag ól.
(Choose your company before you go drinking.)

Ask any foreigner what they associate with Ireland, and they're likely to say 'Guinness' or 'whiskey'. But is the drink a demon or a delight?

We're the first to admit that we enjoy a few drinks, be it the 'Oh, give me a pint' Friday 5 p.m. feeling or the 'Just for the fun of it, I'll polish off a bottle of wine' on a Wednesday afternoon. It's a laugh, and thoroughly enjoyable at the time, but nothing comes without a price in this world. There's the thundering head the morning after, and what drinker has never sworn 'never again'? There are also the things we shouldn't have said and, worse still, the things we shouldn't have done. Inhibitions decrease as the alcohol intake increases. This can lead to one-night stands that may be regretted the following morning, as well as all the other outrageous things we tend to do when we overdo it on the drink.

I asked some of the more talkative interviewees what they felt about drink, and the drinking scene in Ireland. The replies were very mixed. I found that younger people love going out and getting locked, whereas when you get older you tend not to cope with late nights so well, and the desire to get drunk arises less frequently.

> Of course you make a complete fool of yourself when you're drunk. I've shifted guys when I was drunk that I wouldn't touch with a barge pole if I was sober. But isn't that what it is all about?
> GERALDINE, 29, AN ACTRESS FROM GALWAY

There are three particular nights in my life when I have done foolish things with drink on me. At the time I was mortified, but I got over it and now I just laugh at it.
JULIE, FROM LOUTH

The worst thing about getting drunk is that it's great at the time but the suffering you go through the next day is awful. Not to mention when you wake up and remember that you told the local butcher you loved him! There is also the guys you end up with that wouldn't interest you in the slightest when you are sober.

KAREN, 23, AN OFFICE WORKER FROM OFFALY

Going out for a few jars with the lads is one of life's good habits. Better than bad sex any day. And I think when you're single it is the right time to sow all your wild oats – it won't be possible when you have a wife and kids.

STEPHEN, 39, A TRUCK DRIVER FROM CAVAN

I love the drinking scene in Ireland – it's great. Where else in the world would you find so many self-appointed professors of fuckin' everything at 3 a.m. on a Saturday night?

TOM, AN ARTIST FROM KERRY

Let's get to the brass tacks here. What man can honestly say that a night with a woman talking about petty things like emotions or her friends or whatever is more enjoyable than a night on the town with the lads, where you can get as drunk as you want, tell crude jokes and eye up as many women as you want?

TONY, 21, A MECHANIC FROM WATERFORD

I love going out and getting absolutely blocked, especially if I've had a difficult week at work or if I'm mad about something – more often than not it's because some guy didn't phone! Men do it, so why can't we? Regarding things that happen with drink on you, there is no doubt in my mind that unplanned sex is directly related to being drunk. But I become more wary of that kind of thing than when I'm sober.

AMANDA, 23, A SALES ASSISTANT

Girls are easy when they have drink on them, and that is as clear as daylight. Drink definitely makes you randy. I'd head out of a Saturday night with no desire to get a shift, but after seven or eight drinks I'm as horny as bedamned. I'd be attracted to anything in a skirt, and if she's on the way as well, we'll end up together.

NEVILLE, 32, A FARMER FROM DUBLIN

Being drunk gives you a false sense of reality. Everything is either wonderful or appalling, and the opposite sex become so sexy, but I wouldn't give it up for the world. MIKE, 29, A PLUMBER FROM LAOIS

I love going out and getting drunk, it's great craic. Average-looking girls turn into Michelle Pfeiffers, and it's easier to shift them when they are drinking as well.' SÉAN, 25, A SALES REP FROM CORK

One of the most enjoyable things about drinking is heading out with a bunch of your friends and having a few drinks. It can be great fun. All the quiet ones get noisy and all the noisy ones get noisier. We have a right old laugh, joking, slagging and discussing men, and it's all harmless fun. I'm well aware that you can do crazy things with a few drinks on you – what drinker hasn't? I even shifted my cousin! ROISIN, 25, A WAITRESS FROM LOUTH

Drink is probably the best thing about going out. I work long hours and wouldn't drink much during the week, but at the weekends I enjoy my few jars. And not forgetting the vinegar that I consume on Leeson Street! The night wouldn't be the same if I was drinking Ballygowan. I'd get drunk most weekends and once in a while I'll get unconscious – that's when I don't remember how I got home or what I said. I'm sure I've proposed to a fair few women simply because of drink. I hope none of them were stupid enough to take me seriously! JOE, 37, A FACTORY MANAGER FROM DUBLIN

One of the worst things with having a few drinks is getting paranoid. You start imagining all sorts of things and multiplying everything out of proportion. I remember one night I was out with this guy that I had fancied for ages and we ended up going to a night-club together. We were eating the face off each other as we queued to get in. It was great, I was in heaven. With the few drinks, I began thinking of what my cousin preaches to me – 'If you let men walk all over you like a doormat, they'll treat you like a doormat'. So after he had paid in for me and had been kind enough to pay for my coat, I decided to play hard to get. I literally disappeared for half an hour. Talk about doing the wrong thing at the wrong time! When I came back he was innocently talking to another girl, and naturally in my drunken state I thought he was into her, so I freaked it. Needless to say, he didn't want to see me again. ANGIE, 31, A NURSE

I don't drink, and I think the way some people act with drink on them is laughable. The shy types loosen up, and in most cases it doesn't suit them to behave out of character. You know the scene – Paddy, who is a real mummy's boy, is on the town with his mates. Paddy is sporting a freshly washed red rosy face, and a woolly jumper that he got as a present from his mother two Christmases ago. After six or seven pints he has the courage to approach the gang of girls standing beside the pillar. They appear to be having a good time, eyeing up all the available male talent passing by, so Paddy reckons he has a good chance of scoring with one of them. It's pathetic, because he might have some chance if he was sober, but not when he's filled with Uncle Arthur. MARY, 30, FROM CAVAN

I suppose most people who drink are guilty of wearing their 'beer goggles' at some stage. You know what I mean – those nights when you find the four-foot fat-and-frumpy in the corner attractive because you're looking at her through ten pints of Guinness. Luckily, I've never slept with a woman when I was drunk, but a lot of my mates have. That would be something I'd avoid at all costs.
STEPHEN, 33, A SHOP OWNER FROM DUBLIN

A drunk man's mind speaks a sober man's thoughts. I don't drink, and I see it the whole time where people say things with a few drinks on them that they may not have the courage to say when they are sober. MICHAEL, 34, A PUB OWNER FROM MEATH

There's no harm in having a few drinks but, unfortunately, as a single soul you have to be very careful – we don't have anyone there to stop us when we are getting too loud or haul us back when we are jumping into some strange guy's car at three in the morning.
CELINE, 33, AN ESTATE AGENT

The disadvantage with drink is that it's so easy to start and not stop, especially if you're in a round of drinks. There's a constant supply of drink arriving to your table and, like anything, when there's plenty of it around you'll consume it. I have done stupid things I regret with drink on me, including shifting a married man. I didn't know he was married at the time, but I'm sure if I was sober I would have copped on.

I think far too many people go out with the sole intention of getting drunk. That's disgusting in my eyes. Is there anything worse than a drunk man slobbering all over you? It's pitiful. I'd love to video some of the lads some time when they're drunk and play it back to them, 'cause I honestly believe they'd think twice before touching another drink. When I go out with the girls it's invariably to have a few vodkas and get merry. I'd never plan on getting totally twisted – that would ruin the enjoyment of it for me, because more often than not the best nights are the unplanned ones. Getting a snog is all you want after a few glasses, so you'll jump on the first guy you meet. It's a howl.   Mary, a secretary

Having a couple of drinks is enjoyable, you can have the craic and relax. You definitely open up more. The drink does make you randy, and you'll shift anything in a pair of trousers to satisfy your desires at the time. When you wake up sober you invariably regret it.

Emma, 26, a clerk

It sickens me the way people associate Ireland with drink. Big deal. So what if we're partial to a few pints of Guinness – at least we're able to enjoy ourselves, not like the dry shites in America who are beating up their wives, filing for divorce after two months of marriage and screwing their neighbours at the first chance they get. The Irish are a great nation – we know how to have a good time, and that's all that counts at the end of the day. Drunk men can be annoying, but they're not disgusting. And as long as Irish girls don't get themselves pregnant, what harm are they doing?   Declan, 30, from Kilkenny

I think drinking goes in cycles – when you're 18 to 26 or 27, you go out three or four nights a week to get blotto, but as you get older you can't handle the morning after so well, and shifting for the sake of it dies too. It fits in with the general life cycle – at 30 or 40 you should be settled with a wife and kids, so nights on the town aren't as feasible. DERMOT, 37, FROM WESTMEATH

I'd say a lot of one-night stands are drink-related. It's easier when you have a boyfriend there, he'll keep an eye on you and tell you when to stop, but when you're single you rely on your friends, who are invariably just as bad as you.

What annoys me is drunk men. They'll either get all soppy and romantic and tell you you're wonderful and that they love you or they'll get aggressive and start a fight with the other lads. EMILY

Drink has a lot to answer for. I don't think there would be half as many teenage pregnancies if it wasn't for drinking to excess.
PADDY, 30, AN INSURANCE BROKER

Irish men are renowned the world over for their fondness of the black stuff, and I enjoy my pints of Guinness too. But what I can't handle is Irish men who are married to their pint, and would prefer to caress it than you. KATHLEEN, 32, A SOCIAL WORKER FROM WATERFORD

Of course you see things differently with a few jars on you. The men become more attractive – you don't see the wax in their ears or their dirty nails. The danger is that you'd end up doing more than you planned with someone because of being drunk.
MAEVE, A GREENKEEPER FROM MEATH

I'm ashamed to say that yes, I have ended up in bed with a man one night purely because we were both drunk. It's not something I'm proud of. I don't blame anyone but myself, because all my friends were just as bad as I was so they weren't taking any notice of where I was or how I was getting home. That's the risk with drink. As a friend of mine says, it has a taste of more off it. GEMMA, 25, A STUDENT

The worst thing about women drinking is that they can't handle alcohol the way men can. They either puke or cry and it is a nightmare if you are out alone with them.
ANDREW, 23, AN ELECTRICIAN FROM LOUTH

A large percentage of Irish men hit the booze because they're so fed up with life and being single or married, whatever the case may be. It's an easy way out for them. The alcohol helps to block out their thoughts for a few hours.

LINDA, 23, AN OFFICE WORKER FROM LEITRIM.

Women are better at coping with life's little ups and downs, and I don't want men thinking that just because we're women we have smaller ups and downs. Not that at all. We all have work pressures and financial pressures nowadays. Increasing numbers of women are buying their own houses and supporting themselves. Traditionally, it was the man's role to be the provider. I really think it might be a contributory factor in men drinking so much. Women of the nineties don't need men for financial or emotional support any more. And with the sperm banks we won't be needing them at all! In trying to cope with this change, they hit the bottle.

MAURA, 35, FROM KERRY

I was out on a date with a guy once and it was a bit of a disaster. I'd be the first to admit that we didn't get along, but I was quite happy to continue with the night, whereas he hit the bottle in a big way and got totally legless. Being the sort I am, I organised a taxi home for him. I think he hit the bottle because he didn't know how to handle the fact that we didn't get along.

TRISHA, A GRAPHIC ARTIST FROM MEATH

I don't drink much, but all the other lads and girls do and they would get trashed a couple of times a week. Drinking is a huge part of college life. The whole thing of being hungover is seen as something cool. Sometimes, some of the lads wouldn't believe who they actually shifted and it's hilarious to see their faces when they meet up again.

CORMAC, 20, FROM LAOIS

I enjoy my few G&Ts. I go out to have a good time and relax; I'd never go out with the intention of getting completely pissed. Sometimes you can go out and drink all around you and not get drunk, and another night you could just have the one and it would go straight to your head. It all depends on whether you've eaten, the time of the month and what kind of form you're in. I did end up in bed with a guy one night purely because of drink, but I was delighted to wake up and find we both had our clothes on.

MARY, WHO WORKS FOR AN INSURANCE COMPANY

I wouldn't have a lot of confidence in my ability to get a woman, but a few pints gives me great confidence.

SEÁN, 36, A GARDENER FROM MONAGHAN

I'm lucky in that I have the gift of the gab, but I know a lot of lads who drink to get merry and open up. Nowadays, women think they are wonderful – they tease the fuck out of guys and so many women lead men up the garden path. It's unfair, especially when they happen to hit on the quiet lads. Everyone is human and we all have feelings – even men. Take that shocked expression off your face!

GUSSIE, 36, AN AMBULANCE MAN

Believe me, I see it all – girls making passes at me, girls getting sick on the seat; I've even had a chap who pissed on the back seat and he was so drunk I don't think he even noticed. He was a rich kid – nice tin of fruit and lived in Dublin 4. Half the time, there would be couples in the back of the car trying to make out. They'd both be so pissed. It's a panic to listen to them. The funniest was one night the bird had fallen off to sleep, and when it came to paying your man had no money. There he was trying to shake her. I told him to call her. 'I would,' he said, 'but I don't know what the hell her name is!

GEORGE, 45, A TAXI DRIVER FROM DUBLIN

Meeting a Partner

Nuair a stadann an ceol, stadann an rince.
(When the music stops, so does the dance.)

More people are finding it harder to meet people in pubs and discos. No doubt you will have heard your friends complain about how difficult it is to meet a partner. 'Where do you find them?' is a common question. Traditionally in Ireland there were 'Ballrooms of Romance', arranged marriages and matchmakers, and women wouldn't have frequented pubs. But that has all changed now. The majority of people, both men and women, socialise in pubs. I asked some of the interviewees what their views were on the pub and club scene, and where they think people meet partners nowadays.

Some negative comments on the pub and nightclub scene

I can't imagine that I'll meet my husband in a pub or club. Nowadays, pubs and clubs are seedy. For starters you can't hear what people are saying, and in some night-clubs it's almost too dark to see what they look like. CLODAGH, 25, A FACTORY OPERATIVE FROM TIPPERARY

Irish discos are cattle marts. Irish men don't dance – they drink – and Irish girls strut their stuff on the tiles, teasing the mickey off all the lads in sight! JAMES, 27, A SALES REP FROM MONAGHAN

Pubs just aren't the right type of setting to meet people. At weekends they're so packed that you can never manage to get a place beside the man you're chasing, and if you do happen to get standing beside him, please tell me what is the next move. I couldn't imagine just walking up to him and saying 'Hi, I'm Paula'!

PAULA, 31, A FLORIST FROM CLARE

Girls hang around in discos waiting for men to ask them out. The girls will pass by the lads a million and one times in the hope that they'll be noticed. I'd never let my sister go out with any of the lads that I meet at discos.

PADRAIG, A POSTMAN FROM OFFALY

What I hate the most about night-clubs is the way girls refuse offers of dances from lads. Girls will never know what it's like to pluck up the courage to approach them, which means leaving the lads you're with, knowing that every move you make will be scrutinised by them, then try and get the words 'Would you like a dance?' out of your mouth in one go without stammering or stuttering. It's a very difficult thing. And then, as if it's their God-given right to refuse you, they'll coolly say 'No' and proceed to swing their hair into your face. It's an ego-shattering experience – I hate it.

DECLAN, 25, A CIVIL SERVANT

I came across a lovely bunch of lads in Clare who contributed the following. They were all in their early twenties.

Asking a girl to dance is such a wicked chore. When she refuses it's as good as saying 'Fuck off you plonker, who do you think you are, asking me out to dance?' Or worse than that is the 'You're not good enough for me' attitude. We're not saying that we're drop-dead gorgeous, wealthy lads, but we're sound. The more often you get refused, the more upset you become and begin thinking 'Why bother?', so now we don't bother asking girls to dance. It's not worth the confidence deflator that it is.

First impressions are what count at discos. Girls are out to get the tall, dark and handsome types just so that they can compare notes with their friends the following day, so if you are not blessed with good looks, you haven't a hope in hell of getting a girl.

* * *

I'm a shy type of bloke and I find it very hard to meet girls. I've only ever asked two girls out to dance and they both refused, so I don't do it anymore. I'd love if a girl asked me out, but I don't suppose that will ever happen. BARRY, 21, A BARPERSON FROM WICKLOW

Most of the time people are with their friends in pubs and aren't interested in 'picking up' someone. If you do happen to get a glance or a smile from someone, the whole dilemma of guessing what night-club they're going to is the next hitch. It's awful.

RACHEL, 25, A RECEPTIONIST FROM DERRY

Discos are horrible places. Aside from the dark, smoky, noisy atmosphere, very few lads go to discos to get a woman. I think the majority go for more drink – if they can pluck up enough Dutch courage to get a woman, great, but it's not their initial plan.

KATHLEEN, 32, A SOCIAL WORKER FROM KILKENNY

Night-clubs are not conducive to meeting people. People automatically associate night-clubs with shifting or pulling girls, so where does that leave us? If we say no to a dance they complain, and yet most of the time they can hardly string a sentence together.

LIZZIE, 27, AN UNEMPLOYED DESIGNER

When you're young you can't beat the local disco or rugby club for the craic, but as you get older it's definitely more like hard work. Last year, it was all off with my boyfriend of four years, so myself and two girlfriends headed out for the night. I hadn't been out at a disco for years. I really couldn't get over the change. All these young skinny girls half-dressed, dancing to weird rap music. I pestered the DJ to play a bit of Abba, but no joy. So I had to try to dance to songs I didn't know the words to. It was driving me insane – the place was packed, they were blowing out all that white smoke and I couldn't hear a thing. So there I was with my friends on the dance floor. Beside me were a gang of 18- or 19-year-olds. One girl had clogs on her and kept pounding them up and down and stamping her feet on the floor. It annoyed me so much that I nudged her on the elbow and told her to keep the noise down. It was only then I realised that I was definitely getting too old for discos. SUZANNE, 30, FROM KILDARE

It's so funny that you are asking me this question, because just last night eight of us were having a bite to eat in Siobhan's house. Needless to say, the discussion revolved around men. We decided that it is now the era of introduction, because chances are far higher that you'll meet someone through someone rather than in a pub or night-club. Nowadays, it's safer and easier to meet people through people. I think it has got to the stage in Irish society that you can't trust people the way you could in our parents' time. God only knows who you could meet in a night-club and, believe it or not, Galway is such a small city. There is really only the hospital and the army, as the university students are too young. Everybody knows everybody, and if you shift someone from the hospital, everybody knows about it by 11 a.m. on Monday.
MICHELLE, 31, A MIDWIFE FROM GALWAY

As you get older, discos become unbearable. They are great if you are just out for a shift, but to meet a partner – no.
PATRICIA, 32, A SECRETARY FROM GALWAY

I hate the queuing to get in – the obnoxious bouncers that just love refusing you or, worse still, when the 20 people ahead of you get in and then you're stopped and told to hang on. So you end up freezing in the cold for another 20 minutes. Then you'll pay £7 to get in for 30 minutes of crap music, a closed bar and drunken men falling at your feet. SINÉAD, 27, A NURSE FROM DOWN

'Discos are great, but the bad thing about discos is when you're rotten drunk and gagging for a girl. When the slow set comes on, you can never find her so you get really frustrated. When you do find her, she's more than likely eating into some fella's face. Then you become desperate and fall around the place asking every girl in sight for a dance. JOHNNY, 19, A STUDENT FROM MEATH

You don't know who you are picking up in a disco. I know you are taking your chance with anyone, but in a disco you're onto a loser. I am a straight-up type of guy – no strings attached – and I would prefer to meet a woman in the sober light of day. Night-clubs are just glorified cattle marts, with the men hanging on the ring side trying to pick up the beefiest girl on show.   CON, 30, A FARMER FROM SLIGO

I suppose discos are very false – everybody just looks at your face and body, and judges from that. As a teenager, I suffered with acne and it was horrible. Nobody who has clear skin will ever know what it is like to have spots. Girls just ignored me completely.
LIAM, 24, FROM LIMERICK

You would wonder really how the hell we do it. We force ourselves to sit in loud smoky pubs from 9 or 10 till midnight and then bail out, queue for a taxi, queue to get into a night-club, drink more plonk, listen to more bullshit and then queue for a taxi that never arrives. You get home at 5 in the morning absolutely wrecked – pathetic, when you think about it like that.
BRIAN, A MECHANIC FROM LIMERICK

Pubs and clubs are too false. Women and men are not dressed the way they normally dress, and they are also acting out of character. For example, people are different with drink on them and some people only smoke when they go out.   STEWART, 35, A BUSINESSMAN FROM CORK

There's nothing worse than going to a pub that is thronged with teenagers – that for me is a complete turn-off. I think people are drinking at a much earlier age than when I was in my teens. Worse than that is the fact that everybody has become so image-conscious. It's false. I was in the new café-style pub in Cork last month and it was like a breath of fresh air – it had a real relaxed atmosphere and wasn't a bit smoky, plus you could also hear what the people were saying.   PATRICIA, 28, FROM MAYO

People are drunk in discos and it is impossible to have a real conversation with them. This obsession with getting totally twisted – it's a bit like they are all trying to block out life. I can't handle them – they are depressing. Who in their right mind would want to get dressed up and head into a packed, dimly lit club to fill themselves up with beer that is as good as piss and fall out at 3 in the morning with a thundering headache, £30 poorer?'   PETER, 29, A TILER FROM WESTMEATH

I am a firm believer in knowing a girl's background. It says so much about her. To put it bluntly, if I was choosing a bull for my cows I would want to choose a first-class one. It's not snobbiness, just class integration, and you have a higher chance of picking a needle out of a haystack than you have of picking a bird in a night-club. Give me the *Farmer's Journal* meeting column any day.

SÉAN, 34, A FARMER FROM KERRY

Some comments from people who enjoy pubs and clubs

I enjoy going out to pubs – there's nowhere else really to go. I'd always meet my friends there and we have a bit of a laugh. I'd never go to a pub to get a man. If I fancied someone I'd follow him to a disco, but I wouldn't go looking for one in a pub. I've been to a few pubs down South and they are different – the men seem to be quite drunk and they're always packed.   CAROLINE, 23, A STUDENT FROM ANTRIM

You can't beat the craic in Dublin pubs on match nights – they're great sport. Everybody is in a good mood and, especially if France are over, the town is just buzzing.   CELINE, 33, AN ESTATE AGENT

I enjoy discos. If you're out with a gang of friends, discos can be a great laugh. I met my last boyfriend at a disco, in fact.
VALERIE, 22, FROM LOUTH, WHO WORKS FOR A FOOD COMPANY

I love going to night-clubs because I'm mad about dancing, so a gang of us will always head out for a good old bop.
MANDIE, 24, A SHOP ASSISTANT FROM DUBLIN

I think it's great the way there are bar extensions in some pubs today. It means you can sit and relax, have a few beers and not worry about having to move somewhere else come 12 o'clock.
BILLY, 26, AN ELECTRICIAN FROM CARLOW

I go out every Friday and Saturday night, and I always go to my local – I thoroughly enjoy it, 'cause I know all the lads there and we have a right old laugh. If there are any good-looking women about we might pass a comment at them, but that's about it. I'm not interested in meeting a woman at the moment. I'm happy as long as I get me few pints.

ANDY, 31, A PLUMBER FROM OFFALY

It all depends on what you're looking for. If I was looking for a boyfriend, I'd go to where he drinks and do my best to get chatting with him. If I was out for the night, as in a late session, I'd go to a club. However, most weekends I'm just out to meet my friends and catch up on all the gossip. There's no way I'd be able to sit in on a Saturday night, 'cause then it would feel like I didn't have a weekend. To me it's important to socialise, and I'm very content with the social scene in Ireland. Granted, I wouldn't like to think that I'd be still going to discos when I was 30 or 40! *(Thanks Doreen!)*

DOREEN, 25, FROM OFFALY

I think socialising in Ireland is just the same as anywhere in the world. People are out to enjoy themselves, be it to get drunk, to get a shift or whatever. Naturally, you're going to get dressed up to go out. You'd hardly expect me to have come out in my pyjamas tonight would you? Pubs and night-clubs are where most people go to at weekends, so it's the thing to do. There are nights when things don't go as planned – you mightn't get into the club you wanted to, or you might have a fight with one of the lads, but that's all part of it.

JIM, 27, A PHYSIOTHERAPIST FROM MEATH

I love the social scene in Ireland. Irish people have a spirit in them – there is very obviously a passion for life there. I've travelled the world over, and you can't get the same type of craic from any other nationality. To me, Irish men and women are first class. They know how to enjoy themselves, and that's what it's all about. As I've said, I'm of the Leeson Street era and I wouldn't miss it for the world.

JOE, 37, A FACTORY MANAGER FROM DUBLIN

It can be a bit of a drag after a while – you get tired going to the same places and meeting the same people. A gang of us always head away every two months or so to Galway or Kerry and have a great old weekend. You'd get a shift no problem, and you can get as drunk as you want without having to worry about the neighbours catching you.   TANYA, 27, A CHILD-CARE WORKER FROM DUBLIN

Festival time is always a great time. There are bar extensions and there's usually a fair amount of strange girls around the place. It's nice to have a change from the usual scene.
MARTIN, A BUILDER FROM KERRY

Being single when your friends are all going out with people can be a bit of a drag. They'll usually be happy to just go to the pub for a few drinks and then head home, whereas I'm always game to go to a night-club.   RAY, 29, A COMPUTER PROGRAMMER FROM TIPPERARY

It all depends what you want to do socially – there's loads to do, and it is nice to take a break from the pub and disco scene now and then because it does get boring. The cinema is enjoyable, but from the point of view of meeting people I wouldn't recommend it.
GER, 38, A TEACHER FROM DERRY

Most people are happy going to the local at the weekends, but it can get very boring if you go there all the time. A party or a special occasion is always good. From the point of view of meeting a boyfriend or girlfriend I think the whole scene has become too false – the cattle-mart culture has injected an element of sleaze into the club scene. If you are looking for a partner there is a far higher chance that you will meet one outside of the pub and club, maybe in work or in a sports club. Drama groups are supposed to be particularly good meeting spots. Or, better still, meeting people through people – it's easier and more reliable. I actually met my last girlfriend in a supermarket. I read somewhere that singles should do their food shopping on a Friday or Saturday night, as the chances of meeting someone are high.   PAT, 35, A DENTIST FROM MAYO

It's a habit, I think – getting ready on a Friday or Saturday night to head off to the local. You'll meet up with all your friends, and it's the noise and the smoke that makes the atmosphere. If something new took off, like those café bars, I suppose it would only be a matter of time before everybody would start going there. It's just that there is very little else to do at the weekends in a town this small, and I suppose in the back of my mind I'm always hoping that the door will open and my sweetheart will walk in. IAIN, 31, AN ELECTRICIAN FROM KERRY

It all depends what tickles your fancy – night-clubs are great craic, but not all the time. There are a lot of different pubs around nowadays, so you have a great choice. If you feel like going somewhere trendy, it's possible; if you fancy a quiet drink with a friend there's plenty of these pubs too. I think you'll do whatever suits your mood at the time. ANTHONY, 33, A FORESTER

Pub tradition in Ireland will never die. Once you get the taste of them you find it very hard to leave them. Loads of couples that I know have met in pubs, and I think that will be the way for a good while. JACK, 37, A FARMER FROM THE MIDLANDS

It all depends – I'd be wary of a lad I met in a night-club, but I wouldn't decide not to meet him again simply because of that. Loads of my friends met their partners at clubs and are still going strong. Some clubs would definitely be seedier than others – I mean certain places have a name for attracting married men or very young people. It all depends what you want, and as long as you are sober enough to decide, you can head to somewhere with a bit of an atmosphere. SUE, A CRÈCHE OWNER FROM DUBLIN

We all go to different places the whole time. It gets boring when you go to the same place all the time. Variety is good, and Temple Bar is a hot spot at the moment. On a night out we've often just popped our heads into pubs to see what the talent was like, and if it wasn't up to scratch we'd move on. Whereas men are probably happy to go to the same place the whole time. Recently, a gang of us have been sitting in with a couple of bottles of wine and just chatting or eating. It makes for a good change and breaks the routine of the pub and club scene. GRAINNE, 28, A TEACHER FROM DUBLIN

Sitting in your own sitting room with a few cans is about as enjoyable as sex on your own. The thing about going out is meeting your friends, catching up on the latest craic and also the fear that you'll miss out on something. Much and all as we may hate the smell of smoke on our clothes, or the banging noise in your ears after a disco, you can't beat it for the fun. Falling into bed at four or five in the morning makes for an interesting life style. Stories for the grandchildren and all that when you're older.

TIM, 29, A BANKER FROM ROSCOMMON

The whole thing of meeting people, chatting to people, having a slag or a bet or whatever the case may be. It would be boring to go to work five days a week and go to bed with a hot water bottle seven nights a week. That's for the nuns and priests, but not for young single people.

PAUL, 36, A SECURITY GUARD FROM MAYO

Where are single souls to meet that 'special other'?

Outdoor pubs like this one are much more informal – look how easy you got talking to me. There is that feeling of roominess. Of course, there is also the feeling of escape!

JACK, 25, A FACTORY WORKER FROM MEATH

I think parties are a brill idea. Everyone knows everyone, so there is no risk of meeting dodgy characters. I think dinner parties are great – not real posh formal ones but relaxed ones. I live in a house with four other single people, and last Halloween we had a 'murder mystery' party and it was brill. In fact we all got a shift out of it.

JULIE, 27, A DRESSMAKER FROM DUBLIN

I am a firm believer in meeting people through people. For example, I know my mates well and therefore I'd have a fair idea what their sisters would be like. More importantly, their sisters' friends. Joe's sister has a fine-looking bunch of friends. That is the reason I'm here tonight.

DERMOT, 24, A FARMER FROM CAVAN

Night-clubs are grand if you are out for a shift, but not for a relationship. I wouldn't trust a girl I met at a night-club. Anyhow, most of them are too drunk to remember who they have met.

TONY, 30, A VET FROM LIMERICK

Ireland is changing, and about time too. Look at every other European country – they don't have a social scene like ours. In France and Spain you can sit and relax in a smoke-free café for hours. You'll be able to hear the people, and there is none of this Irish mentality where the men want to gulp down as many pints as they can before closing, and where the women are on the hunt for the richest man they can find.   PAULA, 31, A SOLICITOR FROM WEXFORD

It all depends on what you are looking for – even the cool ones in our gang get bored with discos after a while. I think in bigger towns and cities things are more organised, especially for the teenagers. In small towns like this it's almost impossible to do anything but go to the pub or disco. If there were more teen centres like they have in England, I don't think half the young people would be drinking cider down by the canal. From the point of view of meeting people, you'll probably meet them when you least expect it. I wouldn't recommend going out specifically to meet a partner.

SARAH, 31, A HAIRDRESSER FROM WICKLOW

Parties and barbeques, or even outdoor pubs, are far more relaxing atmospheres. There is no pressure to chat up. A party usually brings friends of friends together, so you automatically have a good start for a conversation. Sometimes all that is needed is conversation, and if you are getting along you can take it from there. But conversation is just out of the question in a pub or a disco.

RACHEL, 31, FROM DUBLIN, WHO IS SELF-EMPLOYED

Parties are class – I love them. You are bound to know a good few people, and there is none of the pressure of a disco, where you feel the girls are just waiting to be asked out to dance. For example, in a house party a gang of you can just dance and there is usually just the one dancing area, so everybody joins in.   SEÁN, 32, A BUTCHER FROM SLIGO

I think too many people expect to meet people in night-clubs and pubs. You have a far higher chance of meeting someone at a gym or in work.   FIONA, 32, A CLERK FROM WESTMEATH

Fitness clubs or any type of social club are good meeting places. Night-clubs attract all sorts, good and bad, and you haven't a clue what their background is like, but with sports clubs you have something in common from the start.   CONOR, 32, A GENERAL OPERATIVE

Gyms are more relaxed. I know the sight of my white flesh in a pool with my hair pulled under a swimming cap is not the most attractive sight in the world, but at least everybody is dressed the same and it is only natural to feel embarrassed and paranoid. I've got chatting to more men in steam rooms than I ever would in a night-club. Unfortunately, none of them have asked me out.
   LAURIE, 21, AN AIR HOSTESS

Too many people are caught up with trying to find Mr Right or Mrs Right. What they should be looking for is Mr or Mrs Right Time. Basically, what I mean is that most people meet a fair few people that they could be compatible with, but it may not be the right time. For example, he may be keen on settling down and you won't be, or vice versa.   FIONA, 32, A TEACHER FROM TYRONE

So many people go out at weekends with the specific goal of finding a partner. It is ludicrous. Just like going out to a shop for an outfit for a special occasion – you never find what you want, but if you happen to be just strolling past the shops the chances are far higher that you will find something. Things happen when you least expect them to, especially where romance is concerned. People should just go out for enjoyment, be it to have a few drinks or a bop. But not to find a partner. With age, you get the sense not to feel obliged to head on to night-clubs at midnight when you would prefer to go home to your bed. You don't need to justify this to anybody, especially if you don't enjoy it. Life is too short to feel compelled to go out just so as you won't be known as a dry shite.
   BARBARA, 29, AN ARTIST FROM LIMERICK

> I know loads of people who have met their partners through clubs. Charity walks and hill-walking are especially good. The people have a common interest to begin with, so they can take it from there.
>
> MURT, 33, A FITNESS INSTRUCTOR AND PART-TIME BOUNCER FROM DONEGAL

Conclusion

I was surprised at the number of people who are fed up with pubs and night-clubs. Personally, I loved the old rugby club – it was mighty craic. But I'd be the first to admit that as I get older I find discos become a chore. The interesting thing is that a lot of people agree that love will come along when you least expect it – it's certainly not something that you can go out and buy. However, who said we couldn't increase our chances, and then leave the rest up to Cupid?! It looks as if sports clubs, evening classes, work or being introduced through a friend of a friend provides a far better opportunity than the pub or night-club for meeting that special someone.

7 Blind Dates and Dating Agencies

Is é lár do leasa an tráth is measa leat.
(What you least like is best for you.)

Every week in Ireland, hundreds of people give over their personal details and a contact number to dating agencies and 'lonely hearts' columns in search of a partner. Open any newspaper – national or provincial – or any magazine, and you are bound to find a lonely hearts column that gives details of what the person is looking for and a little bit about themselves. They even have a unique set of abbreviations – soh = sense of humour, tt = teetotaller, ns = non-smoker, and so on. I asked the interviewees for their views on dating agencies and blind dates. Their views regarding the former were negative – only 20% would even consider going to one. 'They are for people who are desperate' was the most common reply. No interviewee admitted that they ever used a dating agency or a lonely hearts column. However, blind dates are seen in a more positive light. Quite a few people – about 15% – have actually gone on a blind date.

Here's what some of the interviewees had to say

> Bad and all as it may be to be single, I'd never go to a dating agency. I suppose I associate it with people who are desperate. It definitely wouldn't be my cup of tea.   MANDIE, 23, A SALES ASSISTANT

I associate dating agencies with people who are desperate to find a partner. I have never thought about going to one, and I wouldn't like to think that I'll ever have to.   PAULA, 24, FROM MEATH

I might as well pay for a prostitute as join up with an agency.
    DERMOT, 34, A FACTORY WORKER FROM LIMERICK

Maybe in a couple of years if I was still single I'd go to one, but not now.   JOANNE, 34, FROM KERRY

I think what's for you won't go by you. When you are ready to meet the right person, he or she will come along. I believe in destiny, and I wouldn't go to a dating agency to find a man.

ANNE, 27, A FARMER FROM WICKLOW

I've never really thought about them, but I wouldn't go. I'd prefer to remain single than reply to an advertisement in a newspaper.

CONOR, 39, FROM CORK

Maybe I'm old-fashioned, but I just think that people who go to dating agencies and write away to lonely hearts columns are very sad and lonely individuals. Desperate, I suppose. I'd hope to meet Mr Right some day, but not through a dating agency.

AOIFE, 40, A MIDWIFE FROM DUBLIN

I suppose it's more a sign of weakness than anything else, the fact that you didn't succeed in finding someone by yourself. A friend of mine replied to a *Farmer's Journal* ad one time, and they're still together. That would be as far as I'd go.   DECLAN, 31, A FARMER FROM MAYO

I just think of a Sunday afternoon, sitting at home reading out the lonely hearts columns and having a laugh at them. I could never imagine writing in to one or replying to one. I often wonder what these people look like. Have they no friends or personality? It's sad.

RORY, 33, AN ARCHITECT

I think it ties in with society's obsession of wanting everybody attached at the hip to someone. Too many people are searching for a partner thinking it will transform their lives – it won't. Being too desperate to meet someone won't bring you to them. You'll meet them when you are good and ready.   STEPHEN, 33, A SHOP OWNER FROM DUBLIN

Sad, lonely people who don't a have a life – that was my first thought when you mentioned dating agencies.   KATHY, 28, A TEACHER FROM LAOIS

The worst thing would be the embarrassment of having to admit to your friends that you met up in an agency. Could you imagine if it worked out and you were getting married, what a slagging you'd get? It wouldn't be worth it. Eddie, 32, from Dublin

There's just something dodgy about them – I can't put my finger on it, but it's not something I'd be interested in doing. Then again, I'm paranoid about everything, so I wouldn't be able to cope with what my friends would think. Siobhan, 22, a bar person from Tipperary

Love is not a tangible object – it's a feeling. You can't go out and buy love like you'd go out and buy a car or a house. I'm totally against dating agencies and these sad individuals who write in to 'meeting place' or whatever. Sending in details about yourself is literally like selling yourself – it's sick. Seán, 30, a garda from Monaghan

I think the lonely hearts columns are particularly risky. Some of them are free, so God only knows what types you could meet. For all you know they could be axe murderers or rapists. I definitely wouldn't reply to any of them.
Shauna, 28, an accounting technician from Waterford

The *Sunday Times* has a dating column and, I must admit, some of the men sound particularly attractive: self-made millionaires and all that, but when it comes to the crunch I'd never pick up the phone or write away. Jane, 34, a beautician from Carlow

They are the kind of things you joke about. The ones in *In Dublin* are a great laugh, and those in the *Farmer's Journal* are a complete panic – 'Genuine farmer with 100 acres and a large milk quota wants to meet nice attractive girl'. As a joke, we sent one in to the *Farmer's Journal* for a friend of ours. It was a howl. She was absolutely mortified – we even enclosed a photo of her when she was topless on a beach in the Canaries. She'll never forgive us.'
Frieda, 31, from Clare

It's a sad reflection of today's society that people are advertising themselves in papers and magazines. It would really make you wonder what is happening to the natural process of accidentally bumping into Mr Right or Mrs Right.

AARON, 23, A FACTORY WORKER FROM LOUTH

I know in India the arranged marriages have a higher success rate, but I'd like to think that the man for me will just appear. I wouldn't like to pay to find him.

ANN-MARIE, 31, A VET FROM THE SOUTH

I'd think of poor unfortunates who can't find somebody by themselves. It's wrong in my view – not natural. If I was left on the shelf at 40 or 50 then maybe I'd consider it, but not now – I'm having too much fun.

TRACEY, 21, A SHOP ASSISTANT FROM LONGFORD

I've never really given them much thought – kind of like 'fine for other people, but not for me'. Maybe for separated or widowed people it's a good idea, but I think young people should be well able to find themselves another half without having to pay for it.

SEÁN, 31, A CAR SALESMAN FROM DONEGAL

Some of those advertisements in the *Evening Herald* would turn you off. I would personally be too afraid of meeting up with a sex-mad pervert or a drug addict or something.

KATE, 30, FROM CAVAN

Bad and all as discos can be, at least you've bumped into them by chance. I don't think you can force an issue like love. If you're destined for someone, you'll meet them in normal circumstances.

MICHAEL, 23, WHO WORKS IN A HARDWARE STORE

Dating agencies are the type of thing that I would automatically associate with shy people or people with no personality.

JOE, 37, A FACTORY MANAGER FROM DUBLIN

Whatever about dating agencies, sending in personal stuff to a newspaper is awful. You haven't a clue what kind of weirdo they might be.

LINDA, 23, A DRESSMAKER FROM ANTRIM

Here are some of the positive replies

❝ I see nothing wrong with them at all. I don't feel strongly enough about having a girlfriend to go to one at the moment, but if and when I do feel like a partner I'll have no problem in joining an agency. I think a lot of people are too self-conscious to go to one – it's as if they can't cope with the idea that they have to get help to find a partner. But when you think about it, you are taking a bigger risk with dating someone you meet at a disco. You don't know anything about them, their past, etc. At least with an agency, you'll know the important things about them like interests, job, etc.

DERMOT, 37, A CHEF FROM WESTMEATH

A friend of mine joined up with an agency last year, and he has had a ball. They have organised about ten dates for him, some of which worked out and some which didn't, but he really enjoys it. He is separated and found it very difficult to meet a woman.

JAMES, 28, FROM DUBLIN

It all depends on the person – if somebody is separated or has just returned from working abroad, then it makes sense to join an agency to meet new people and do different things. It's no fun living on your own forever. What I wouldn't be in favour of is people just rushing off to an agency for fear of being left on the shelf. It is harder to meet people in pubs and clubs, and you're taking a risk with anything. But people should be happy with whatever status they are. Never feel pressured into getting a husband or a wife – you'll be married for long enough!   MIKE, 26, A QUANTITY SURVEYOR FROM WEXFORD ❞

Here are some of the comments regarding blind dates

❝ Blind dates can be a bit of craic. I went on one once and it was a complete disaster. The two of us were so nervous that we weren't acting naturally. There was pressure to impress, and it didn't work. But I'd go on one again no problem.

CAROLINE, A PUBLIC RELATIONS EXECUTIVE FROM DUBLIN

As I get older, more and more of my friends are getting married, with the result that they are constantly fixing me up with people. When blind dates are taken in a lighthearted fashion they can be great, but if you get too caught up with them they are a disaster. A lot of my friends are always saying, 'God, Lee, I met this guy in work who's single, and he'd be perfect for you'. When I do finally get to meet him, he's invariably not my type at all.

LEONIE, 35, FROM OFFALY

The worst thing about blind dates is when it comes to meeting the person for the first time. My friends fixed me up one time, and I told the girl that she'd be able to recognise me 'cause I'd be the one wearing a baseball cap. As I was walking into the pub, I felt like a complete spa so I took the cap off and left it on the bar counter. The girl walked into the pub, had a look for a guy with a baseball cap and left. Funnily enough, we met up about a week later and we went out together for six months. We often joked about the baseball cap, and she reckons we wouldn't have got it together if I had been wearing it.

JOE, 27, FROM LIMERICK

The one and only time I went on a blind date was a complete disaster. We were both really outgoing and chatty people, so neither of us got a word in edgeways. From then on I've become a firm believer in 'opposites attract'!

ANGELA, 28, A PRODUCTION WORKER

A friend of mine had a singles dinner party one time. The guy I fancied ended up fancying her, and the guy she fancied had the hots for me. Neither of us got a shift that night. It was hilarious, because the more I tried to impress my fella, the more he fancied her, and vice versa.

MARY, 23, A 'COMPUTER FREAK'

I think it all depends. Sometimes you meet someone, maybe at work or something who would be single and you'd think he would be perfect for your friend, but when they get together they just don't bond at all. I think you try too hard to impress, and it doesn't work like that.

FIONA, 30, A BANKER FROM DUBLIN

A bit like the time I went to a blind date ball. I was given a pink bracelet with a number on it, and had to find the guy wearing a blue bracelet with the same number. At the start we were on edge, but after a few beers we both relaxed and we got on brilliantly. We actually went out together for a while.   FIONA'S FRIEND, DAILBHE

I'd be way too shy to go on a blind date. It wouldn't be worth it – my nervous system would collapse.   JANE, 27, A NURSE FROM DUBLIN

It would all depend who he was – if it was a friend or brother of somebody I trusted, well and good.
   SUSAN, 19, A STUDENT NURSE FROM LIMERICK

I went on a blind date one time, and it was a laugh from start to finish. John had the same coloured shirt and jeans on as me, and I was fit to kill my friend, thinking that she told him what I was going to be wearing. It turned out that our birthdays were on the same day and that his sister was going out with my cousin. We got on pretty well, but he never asked to see me again. I don't know why.
   EUGENIE, 23, FROM GALWAY

There's nothing worse than blind dates – they are so false. It is such a complete set-up that you act irrationally and out of character. To me, it's like taking a car on a test drive, and that's not what the dating game is about. I'd never agree to go on one.
   STEWART, 35, A BUSINESSMAN FROM CORK

The great thing about blind dates is that they can be a real bit of craic. I remember going on one once. My friend set me up with her brother. It was a scream. We got on famously, but there was no physical attraction there at all. We had a right old laugh at the fact that people thought we'd be good together.
   GERALDINE, 27, A SECRETARY FROM LIMERICK

I've often ended up at business dinners sitting opposite some real babes – a bit like a blind date in a way – and they are great. I remember one time I tried it on with a lady under the table cloth. We were in a really top-class restaurant and I took off my shoe and rubbed my foot along her leg. She screamed 'mouse!' and ended up falling off the chair. I'd no time to put my shoe back on. Needless to say, I was mortified.   JOE, 37, A FACTORY MANAGER FROM DUBLIN

Dating agencies – the facts

Because of the huge negative reaction to dating agencies, I decided to check them out and see exactly what they are, who joins and, most importantly, whether they work. Armed with a list of questions, I went to visit Ireland's leading introduction and social events agency, Who's Who for the Unattached, based in Dublin. Prior to visiting the agency I had mixed views about dating agencies, but the visit changed my whole perspective. As I was approaching the building I was hoping I wouldn't bump into anyone I knew: 'God forbid they should see me going to a dating agency – what would they think?' My attitude was completely reversed when I stepped back out on the street. I couldn't have cared less who saw me.

Who's Who for the Unattached was established in 1991, and there have been 75 marriages as a result of people meeting their partners through the agency. Who's Who organises a variety of social events for members including dinner parties, golf outings, horse riding, holidays, casino nights and much more. Who's Who is constantly growing and expanding. At present it has approximately 3,500 members, ranging in age from 22 to 74.

So, who joins a dating agency?
People have many reasons for joining dating agencies – work is confining, friends are already in partnerships, business is too demanding, it's too much effort to go out looking, and so on. Meeting people in the pub or club is becoming more and more difficult, hence the growth and success of introduction agencies. People have become much more positive and adventurous in their approach to finding a partner. They have decided not to leave it to chance, but to explore all possible avenues.

How does it work?
Every prospective member is personally interviewed and screened, as Who's Who is a personalised dating agency and does not rely on computer matching. All introductions are arranged by a trained adviser who monitors members' success.
    The interview process can take up to two hours, during which time

the consultant and client go through a thorough personality profile outlining the following: personal details, professional details, education, status, hobbies, sporting activities, entertainment interests, personal qualities, general interests, non-sporting activities, ideal holiday, pet hates, favourite foods, weaknesses and strengths, reading interests and other relevant details.

The client is asked to write a paragraph about himself or herself on each of the following:
· who I am
· what I like to do
· what I'm looking for.

The consultant now has an extensive file on this member, with a full personality profile as well as information about the type of person they wish to meet.

The next step is to match profiles. The personal consultant who conducted the initial interview will manage and oversee all introductions.

Once a profile is chosen, the consultant phones each member with the other person's profile. When each party has heard the other's profile and agreed to go on a date, phone numbers are exchanged and a date is arranged between the couple. Needless to say, if Cupid is on your side you might need only the one date!

It appears that the growth of agencies in recent years is a reflection of the general opinion that meeting the person of your dreams is getting harder and harder. Personally, I think that it doesn't matter how you meet or what method you use to increase your chances of meeting that special person, as long as you are happy. If you are content to live a single life, all the better.

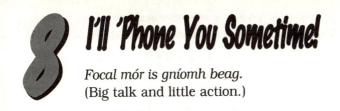

8 I'll 'Phone You Sometime!

Focal mór is gníomh beag.
(Big talk and little action.)

A lot of girls have at some stage hung around the house waiting in vain for a guy to phone. Your parents know damn well why you're in a bad mood but they don't say anything; your brothers tease you about being a fool, but you tell them to feck off and leave you alone. Why the hell didn't he phone, you ask yourself – he was all on for it last night. He even went to the bother of getting a pen from the barman! You console yourself with the idea that he lost it – maybe he'll phone during the week. The weeks pass, and no call. Why do men take women's phone numbers if they have no intention of phoning them? Are we bigger eejits to give them our numbers? Judging from the results, I think we are!

The following questions were put to the interviewees.

> *Have you ever taken a girl's telephone number and not phoned her? Why?*
>
> *Has a guy ever taken your telephone number and not phoned you? Why do you think they don't phone?*

The results show that 75% of the 454 men always or sometimes take a girl's phone number, depending on the situation, but only 30% actually phone the girl. Of the 60% of the 435 girls interviewed who sometimes give a guy their telephone number, about half are still waiting on a call. As for the reasons why they don't phone – let's just say that I'll never again give my telephone number to a guy!

The guys who take girls' numbers and don't phone...

The most popular replies from the lads for not phoning were 'drink talk', 'pissed at the time' and 'easiest way out'.

> It's an easy way out at the end of the night. When the lights come on and you get a real look at her, it can be a bit of a nightmare sometimes. The quickest and easiest way to get rid of her is to ask her for a phone number. SCOTT, 24, A SOLICITOR FROM DUBLIN

> After a few pints and a shift, it comes naturally to ask a lass for her phone number. PAUL, FROM CORK, WHO IS UNEMPLOYED

> With a few drinks on you, everything is different. If I had to keep all the matchboxes, fag boxes, racecards, toilet paper, you name it with girls' telephone numbers on them, you'd have enough for your whole book. Of course it's great to wake up the following morning with a number scrawled on a piece of paper. But believe me, I'd never ever have any intention of phoning the girl. It's part of the outfit you wear when you're on the town. Not something that you'd do in the day time. BARRY, 29, AN INSURANCE BROKER FROM MAYO

> It depends what you did and how drunk you were. If she made a good impression on me and I had the time during the week, I might give her a call. I suppose girls wouldn't be as drunk as the lads, so they can remember you and if they think you were nice it can be a bit of a blow when you don't phone. Also, if she was a bit of a laugh and wasn't too giving of herself you might be keen to pursue her. EAMONN, 34, A BUILDER FROM TIPPERARY

> The five rules of single life are simple: Five Fs. (1) Few beers, (2) Few short ones, (3) Find bird, (4) Fone and (5) Forget. It's a challenge to get a girl's phone number – I find the older birds are throwing it out, whereas the younger ones are catching on to us a bit. I went around a night-club one night and collected ten phone numbers from girls and won myself a tenner. The following day one of the lads bet me £100 that at least one of the numbers was bogus. It was a panic –

I didn't have a clue what any of the girls' names were. A young lad answered the first number, so I asked him if his sister was there. When he said 'Which one?' I said 'The one who was at Big Eddie's disco last night'. 'Oh yeah, Maura – hold on.' It was easy, so I continued. I was on number eight, and I'll never forget it – the number was (01) 6771425. Dublin Zoo. I'll never forget it – it cost me £100 and a slag for the rest of my life.   RICHIE, 30, FROM MEATH

It's the easiest way to end a night. If I've shifted a bird and she's hanging around and I'm worried that I might miss my lift home, I'll ask her for her number, which they are always so willing to give. She then scurries off like a cat who got the cream, and it's great.
GARY, 29, A BARMAN FROM DUBLIN

I'm forgetful.   DAMIEN, 30, A DEVELOPMENT OFFICER FROM TYRONE

It can be a drag when there's a girl tagging on to you at the end of the night when all you want to do is go home to your bed alone! The simplest thing is to ask her for her phone number. You'll have made her day, and she'll leave you alone.   TURLOUGH, 24, A FACTORY OPERATIVE

Generally, I don't take a girl's number. If I happen to get a shift at a disco, that's all it would be. I wouldn't have any mad desire to meet her again. It satisfied my need at the time, and that was great. But, on the other hand, if I met a girl and there was something different about her that I really liked –maybe even the fact that she was a good kisser – then I'd definitely take her number and phone her.
MARTIN, 24, A PLUMBER FROM SLIGO

A phone call is more than just a phone call – it means you're interested in seeing this person again and that's serious, so you would need to have your wits about you. You're hardly going to phone and say 'Hi, how's the weather in your back garden today?'
JERRY, 25, A NURSE FROM WATERFORD

A night out means freedom, having a laugh, and a shift is the icing on the cake. It certainly isn't a profession of a guy's undying love for you when he takes your number – it's the drink talking.
KEVIN, 28, FROM DUBLIN

I'd say most guys have no idea what they are doing when they are taking a girl's telephone number. It's the easy way out. Girls would be fools if they sat beside the phone waiting for a lad they met at a disco to phone. Bimbos. STEPHEN, 33, A SHOP OWNER FROM DUBLIN

I never phone because my brother always takes my T-shirts and puts them in the washing machine. JAMES, 23, A GARDA FROM CLARE
(Quite a few witty lads had the same reply!)

I probably forgot her name. Had all the intentions at the time of phoning her. But then I might have been doing something else or never thought of it, or whatever. BRIAN, 32, A FACTORY WORKER FROM DONEGAL

As a rule, I don't take women's numbers. The odd time I might wake up after a night on the town with a number scribbled on an empty cigarette box, but I'd hardly ever remember who the hell she was or what she looked like. JOE, 37, A FACTORY MANAGER FROM DUBLIN

Some lads are just out to get a shift; others are out for more. It all depends – if you're happy with what you got, you'll ask for a number and she's gone. It's easy. To be blunt about it, some girls are just dying for a man to ask for their number so, to satisfy your conscience seeing as how you've just used this girl for what you could get, you'll ask her for her number. At least that way her night will have been successful. I've never phoned a girl. I've taken a fair few numbers in my heyday. It's all part of the singles game.
ANDREW, 35, A TECHNICIAN FROM OFFALY

The best craic is getting one of the other lads to phone and pretend it's you. We do it the whole time and it's priceless, especially when you start telling her what a good kisser she was and what a great time you had! TONY, 21, A MECHANIC FROM WATERFORD

If a woman has a unique approach, it works. One time a girl wrote her number on my socks with a pen, and when I woke up the following day I laughed so I decided to phone her. We actually went together for a few months. JOHN, 34, AN ARMY OFFICER

This fascination with telephone numbers is hilarious. Do girls not know the basic rules of dating and mating? When a guy asks for your number it does not mean that he will phone you – it simply means he is grateful for the shift or the shag or whatever he got, but hey, that's it. I'd really worry for any girls who sit by the phone waiting on guys to call. SEÁN, 29, A BUSINESSMAN FROM KERRY

...and the guys who do phone

I would always phone a girl if I took her number. As I've said, I rarely meet girls in pubs or discos. It tends to be in sober circumstances where we can see and hear each other properly. The way I see it, if they're interested enough to give it to me in the first place and I was interested enough to take it, it's only common courtesy to phone.
MURT, 33, A FITNESS INSTRUCTOR AND PART-TIME BOUNCER FROM DONEGAL

I take phone numbers from girls if I'm interested in meeting them again, and I always phone them. But I have found that when you do phone, it's the girls who aren't interested. It's happened to me twice and I've only ever phoned a girl five times.
COLIN, 24, A FACTORY WORKER FROM KERRY

I'd never take a girl's telephone number unless I was keen on her. I had a girl give me her telephone number one time and it didn't feel right, so I didn't phone her. If I was keen on a girl I would definitely take her number and phone her. DARREN, 36, FROM WATERFORD

You don't want to be too keen either. I always wait a week to ten days and then just when they think they'll never hear from me again I ring. It's worth it to see their reaction. CORMAC, 25, A BUILDER FROM GALWAY

I would always phone a girl if I took her number. But I wouldn't always take it. PAUL, A FACTORY OPERATIVE FROM DONEGAL

I'm a straight-up type of lad and wouldn't lead girls up the garden path. I've often taken numbers from girls and phoned them.
DECLAN, 25, A DEPARTMENT OF HEALTH EMPLOYEE

I never take phone numbers – waste of time.
BARRY, A DELIVERY MAN FROM TIPPERARY

There's no rationale for taking a girl's number. If I was keen enough on a girl I'd arrange to meet her. IAN, 26, FROM KILDARE

What do the girls think of the numbers game?

It's the two at ten and ten at two theory. At ten o'clock a guy might give a girl two out of ten, whereas at 2 a.m. the same girl could get ten out of ten. The whole thing of seeing people in a different light with drink.
LIZANNE, 34, A TEACHER FROM DONEGAL

I genuinely don't know why guys don't phone. They seem so keen at the disco and do their best to get a pen and piece of paper, yet days pass and you never know what's happened.
ROISIN, 27, FROM MEATH

It beats me.
ÁINE, 19, A STUDENT FROM CARLOW

No, a guy has never not phoned me. I think the reason they don't phone is because on the night they're out having the craic, but next day all is back on track and they have forgotten about the girl.
MANDIE, 23, A WAITRESS FROM DUBLIN

The bottom line is that if guys are interested they'll phone – there's no two ways about it.
ANNE, 27, A FARMER FROM WICKLOW

I've gone out with guys that have phoned me so I don't really know if guys don't phone – they always phone me.
CIARA, 23, FROM SLIGO

I had a guy take my phone number one time and he didn't phone because he thought I was into somebody else. They chicken out, basically.
SHAUNA, 32, A PERSONAL ASSISTANT

It's the easiest option, rather than saying 'I don't want to see you again'. I've taken a lad's telephone number and didn't phone him 'cause it was the easiest way out.
DEIRDRE, 29, A CLERK FROM KILKENNY

It's just something to say at the end of the night – a kiss-off, really. I wouldn't give my number.
BARBARA, 28, FROM TIPPERARY

You can give as good as you get – we often give out bogus numbers to lads, and it's a howl. On the night it's great craic and we never have to wonder whether they are going to ring.
AISHLING, 23, A STUDENT FROM CORK

As you get older you cop on to men's games more, and you become more selective about who you give your number to. When you're younger you wait and wait for him to phone, but as you get to know men better you realise that it's just a drink thing to take a girl's number.   FIONNUALA, 32, AN ACCOUNTANT FROM WEXFORD

It's a bit like anything in life – the ones who phone you aren't the ones you want, and you never hear from the ones you fancy.
                                         MAURA, 31, A SALES REP

It all depends on the situation – if you shift a guy in a disco and it was just a once-off thing, you don't expect him to phone. It's nice of him to ask for your number, and you might even give him your friend's number. If you meet a guy at a wedding or at the races and you got on really well, you'd be hoping he'd ask to see you again. I'm more worldly wise now than I was five years ago, so I don't automatically expect men to phone.   SUZANNE, 26, AN ENGINEER FROM SLIGO

One of the best things in the world is when a nice guy that you met actually phones you – it's great.
               ALISON, 33, FROM WESTMEATH, WHO WORKS IN A PET SHOP

Of course phone numbers are now a thing of the past – the latest chat-up is 'what's your e-mail address?' I actually have one, and I met a guy two weeks ago at a party. So we swapped e-mails. On Monday morning I was mortified when I saw that he had written to me. I replied, and now we e-mail each other every day. It's cool. I haven't been officially asked out yet though, but fingers crossed.
                    NOREEN, 29, FROM DONEGAL, WHO WORKS IN COMPUTING

I just can't understand it. Last week I met this lovely man and he even took my address – now please try and explain that one for me.
                         LINDA, 26, A QUALITY CONTROLLER FROM LOUTH

Worse than men who don't phone are weirdos who hound you. I met this guy two years ago at the local disco on a Saturday night, and gave him my number. He rang me on the Sunday and to be honest,

I was surprised. When I saw him in daylight I wasn't interested at all. But he pestered me for ages. My parents weren't at all impressed with the phone ringing at two or even three in the morning.
Nuala, 26, a trainee accountant

I suppose everything is exaggerated with a few drinks – even thinking he was keen. He probably wasn't at all, but with five or six Heineken on you 'What's your number?' translates into 'I'm mad about you!'
Leonore, 29, a marketing executive from Tipperary

If a guy asks me for my number, I take his instead – at least that way the ball is in your court, so if you feel like ringing him you can. No matter what people say, you do subconsciously jump every time the phone rings if you've given your number to a guy, and it's not worth the hassle.
Anita, 34, a lecturer from Waterford

Well, I think the truth has been revealed. Why couldn't our parents have told us this when we were younger? All the heartache it could have saved!

Rules Were Made to Be Broken

Is olc an chearc ná scríobfadh dí féin.
(It's a poor hen who wouldn't scratch for herself.)

Why shouldn't women ask men out? After all, it is the nineties and women can earn their own money, drive their own cars and return to work after having their children. In the sixties and seventies in Ireland, it would have been almost unheard of for a single woman to buy her own house. Most of the mothers I know, including my own, had to give up their state jobs as soon as they had their first child. But that has all changed now.

Today, women are on Boards of Directors, they can become surgeons, solicitors, green-keepers and vets, and even freeze their eggs until they feel the time is right to start a family. However, when it comes to asking men out, women tend to take a back seat.

What do men think of being asked out by women?

The positive views
Only 124 of the 444 women surveyed (28%) have ever asked a man out, whereas 81% of the men would have no problem with being asked out by a woman. I got a huge number of positive replies and brought smiles to hundreds of men's faces at the mere thought of being asked out by a woman.

> I'd be flattered if someone asked me out, but to be honest I don't think it will ever happen.
> SEÁN, 32, A BUTCHER FROM SLIGO

> All my Christmases would come at once.
> MARTIN, A FARMER IN HIS LATE 30S FROM WESTMEATH

> I'd be over the moon.
> DAVID, 24, A TEACHER FROM CARLOW

I would marry the girl who had the intelligence to ask me out. Begorrah, the cards are laid out like this – I have a very big farm, a house, a huge bank balance (that isn't in the red!), and to top it off I'm a solid bloke with plenty of years left in me.

PAT, A FARMER FROM MAYO WHO WOULDN'T REVEAL HIS AGE

I'd be chuffed if a bird asked me out on a date. Me mate had someone ask him out once, and they went out together for months. At first, me mate thought she'd be some kind of a Margaret Thatcher but it turned out that she was more of a Pamela (as in Anderson). I can't see a bird asking me, 'cause I come across too strict – a bit gruff and rough at the edges.

KEVIN, 28, FROM DUBLIN

I don't think women know what they want – one minute they want flowers and dinner and the car door opened for them, the next minute they want to pay their own way and drive their own car. Yet they wouldn't pick up a phone and ask a lad out. If they're as good as men and demand equal pay and all that, why can't they phone? It really galls me the way they go on, and chances are the bloke will never phone them, 'cause he doesn't reckon that he has a chance. Lads aren't as tough as we're made out to be. We don't all think that we can score with any chick that we want. We have our hang-ups too. If I had a quid for all the times I've heard me mates say that women have it easier 'cause they don't have to do the running, I'd be a very wealthy man. My advice to women is fire ahead and ask the lad out. Sooner or later it will all revert back to the old ways, 'cause women will get tired of playing a man's life. Until then, decide who you want and go for it.

ANDREW, 23, AN ELECTRICIAN FROM LOUTH

I would have no problem with being asked out by the opposite sex. I don't see anything wrong with it at all – in fact, my sister, after much persuasion from me, asked Peter out over a year ago and they are still together.

SCOTT, 24, A SOLICITOR FROM DUBLIN

It's only proper for a girl to be able to ask a boy out – it's not as if she's looking for marriage or anything; it's only a date and I say 'fair play to her'.

MIKE, 26, A QUANTITY SURVEYOR FROM WEXFORD

More power to girls who ask men out. I definitely don't think they're desperate or overbearing. It's like this – would you think a chap was desperate to ask you out? The sexes are treated more fairly these days, and that's the way it should be. I deal with a lot of farmers who think it's disgraceful that women can be vets; in fact there are some farmers who won't allow female vets to treat their animals – that to me is downright old-fashioned. I would have absolutely no problem if a girl asked me out. In fact, I might be turned on by the idea. No, forget the 'turned on' bit – don't put that in the book.

JAMES, 29, A VET

Sorry, James – it was too interesting to leave out. (I did leave out where you were from, though!)

Girls have more to lose than gain by not asking lads out – the games girls play are more like crying games. You can never tell where you stand with them – one day they're mad for you, and the next day they're running away from you. It's pure crazy. No insult to you or anything – I know you have all that PMT crap but it's so difficult for us lads to know where we stand with ye. Half the time you'd be afraid to ask a girl out 'cause one minute she's coming on to you big time and you reckon you're in with a chance, and then she's giving you the cold shoulder treatment, so in the end you don't bother asking her out again. She's the loser. What I'm trying to say is that if a girl is mad for a lad then she should go ahead and ask him out, because if he's like me he won't take the risk.

TONY, 21, A MECHANIC FROM WATERFORD

I was asked out by a few women, and ended up dating two of them for a while. I have absolutely no problem with it at all.

MURT, 33, A FITNESS INSTRUCTOR AND PART-TIME BOUNCER FROM DONEGAL

I wish more women would ask me out. I see nothing in the wide world wrong with asking men out, just like I don't see anything wrong with women who initiate sex. Why do men always have to be the trigger-pullers – we have to ask them out, we have to phone them, we have to make the moves. It's unfair.

STEPHEN, 39, A TRUCK DRIVER FROM CAVAN

The negative views

> I'm old-fashioned. I like a woman to be a woman. I pay the bills, I decide where to go and I always decide what movies we see. If a woman asked me out, I'd refuse. To me, it's a sign of desperation. Who the hell does she think she is, assuming in the first instance that I'd be attracted to her and secondly that I'd go on a date with her?
>
> STEWART, 35, A BUSINESSMAN FROM CORK

When Stewart was asked whether he'd ever been asked out, he replied with a very adamant 'no'.

I think men should do the asking. If a woman asked me out, I'd be scared of her – I don't like a domineering woman.' *So just because a woman asks you out, it means she's domineering?* No, not exactly – it's just that I prefer to call the shots.

BRIAN, 26, A BANK OFFICIAL FROM TIPPERARY

I met a lovely girl one night and we swapped phone numbers. A week or so later she asked me out for a drink, and I turned her down. A month later my best friend, John, got going out with her and they're still together. We meet a good bit, and I think I'm more embarrassed than she is. She treats it as a bit of a joke and says 'Look what you missed out on'. Why did I say no to her offer? I really was shocked – it was a Wednesday night and the football was on telly and I thought 'Who the fuck is phoning me?' It really didn't sink in until I'd hung up the phone. I wasn't shy or anything, and I didn't think she was weird. I can say it now because I know her well that she was just out for the craic. But believe me, if a woman ever phones me again to ask me out, even if it's in the middle of a Cup Final, I definitely won't be saying no!

TOM, 24, AN ARMY OFFICER FROM KILDARE

In Wicklow I came across a very interesting bunch of young men and women who contributed the following.

Because men are so used to doing the asking, it is very strange when a woman asks you out. But that feeling of strangeness only lasts for a split second, and then you realise that it is perfectly normal and fine. I think once people get used to the idea it will be readily and easily accepted. Girls have a far higher chance of getting a positive reply from their proposal than men do. I doubt that too many men would refuse a girl's offer to go on a date, whereas a huge number of women think that they can just refuse men the whole time.

Girls on asking guys out

So, girls, why are only 28% of you willing to ask a guy out? The most common reason given was shyness, followed by fear of refusal.

I don't know what it is – it's probably shyness. It's a bit like when you go out for a meal with a guy, and the waiter always gets the man to test the wine. I don't have a problem with that at all, but Sarah, a friend of mine, goes mad. I mean, it's the sort of thing I expect a man to do, and to be honest I'd prefer to go on thinking and dreaming about a guy rather than pluck up the courage to ask him out.
JANE, 27, A NURSE FROM DUBLIN

I would die if I had to ask a man out. I'm a really shy person and find it hard enough to talk to men, let alone ask one out. I don't think there's anything wrong with it – in fact I'd love to be able to do it.
ANNE, IN HER MID-30S, FROM DUBLIN

I would be too shy – I'd have to polish off a bottle of vodka before I even phoned him, and then chances are he'd probably refuse me anyway.
MADGE, 33, A TEACHER FROM MEATH

I'm by nature a very outgoing person, but when it comes to men I don't know what it is – I just freeze up. PAULA, 22, A STUDENT FROM CLARE

I got so tired of listening to my friend Jessica going on about this boy that she fancied that I phoned him myself. I pretended I was Jessica and arranged a date for 8.30 p.m. at the local chipper. I didn't tell Jessica anything until we got to the chipper. Paul was already there, all dressed up and looking well. Jessica was scarlet when she saw who was there. I left the two of them there and went on. Unfortunately, it didn't work out, but Jessica found out that he wasn't the type of guy she thought he was at all. In the end it was worth it. Now, any time Jessica goes on about a guy she's into, I always say 'Chipper, chip' and she shuts up!

RACHEL, 25, A RECEPTIONIST FROM DERRY

I don't know what it is really – probably the fear that he might think I was hard up or something. At the moment I'm mad into a guy who works on the check-in desk, but I'd never be able to ask him out. To be honest, I hadn't even thought about it – you mean like just go right up to him and ask him on a date? *Yes.* God, no – I couldn't do that. I mean, I wouldn't even be able to ask him out to dance in a fast set. I suppose I'm one of those girls who expects the fellow to do the asking. *Do you think he knows that you fancy him?* I don't know – I always make an effort to talk to him and chat about his weekends and stuff, but that's about it. *Maybe he just thinks you're being nice.* Yeah, I suppose, maybe you're right – next time you're doing a survey I might have a totally different attitude. I might even have asked him out!

LAURIE, 21, AN AIR HOSTESS

I would ask a guy out on a date if I was sure he wouldn't refuse, but that's the problem. In the back of your mind you're always thinking negative thoughts, and it wouldn't be worth the embarrassment if he said no.

SUSAN, 19, A STUDENT NURSE FROM LIMERICK

Girls who have asked men out

Any of the girls who have asked a guy out admitted that it was a little nerve-racking at first, but said that it was always brilliant fun. None of them regretted the move.

I was shitting a brick the week before the big deed, and then I went to jelly when he actually came on the phone and I couldn't ask him out at all – it was a panic; my friends were all eavesdropping in the kitchen.

MARY, 22, A STUDENT FROM CORK

I laugh when I think about it – I was so nervous. It was about two years ago and I had been into this chap for ages. Little by little I gathered up some inside information on him – where he lived, where he worked, marital status, etc. The day I managed to get his phone number was a howl – myself and some friends had spotted him coming out of the video shop and this gave us an idea. Clare phoned the video store and let on she was from another video shop and that this particular gentleman had run up huge fines and had left them a bogus address and phone number. Clare then proceeded to ask for a contact telephone number; the video store kindly obliged. I had a list written out on how to cope with all possible outcomes:

(a) he may not be there, so just hang up
(b) answering machine – don't leave a message
(c) woman answers the phone – let on that it's Telecom Eireann checking the call-answering service
(d) he's there – begin with casual chat
(e) move on to 'I was speaking with you very briefly in the pub two weeks ago' – if he remembers, move on to (f); if he doesn't remember, hang up immediately
(f) chat about work, and living in the area
(g) if his replies are brief, finish up with 'just called to see if you were settling in well in your new home'; if replies are long and he seems keen, move to (h)
(h) ask to meet him for a drink.

Then, after a few beers, I dialled his number. It was a complete disaster – for starters he answered the phone immediately, which I wasn't expecting at all. Then I couldn't find what letter I was at on the list, so I began talking about the weather and eventually I just hung up. The girls were in stitches. I started to cry, and then I just went into fits of uncontrollable laughter. It can be great craic if you have the right attitude, look at it as being a bit of fun. I've since asked a few guys out, and I'm no longer shy or nervous about it.

Caroline, a public relations executive from Dublin

I met Eamonn at a festival in my local town. As I'd previously worked with him, we fell into an easy banter. Finding that my feelings had changed towards someone I'd previously seen as a platonic friend, I was anxious to meet up with him again. Leaving myself in a vulnerable position in his local the following weekend, I bumped into him once again. One drink led to another, and eventually myself and Eamonn hit the local night-club, which finished perfectly with a snog, and because I was reluctant to give my phone number to any man, Eamonn gave me his. After careful consideration, I decided that Thursday would be the perfect 'not too keen' day to phone him. The phone call went well and Eamonn promised to ring sometime. Sick of waiting around, I decided a week and a half later that I was going to ask him out, and as it happened a close friend had spare tickets for the Neil Diamond concert. I picked up the phone without giving myself time to think about what I was doing, and dialled.

    Hello.
    Hello, Eamonn – it's Angela here.
    Oh, Angela! Jaysus, sorry I never got a chance to ring you.
    Ah, sure, not to worry.
    So, how are things with you anyhow?
    Great, Eamonn – thanks. Look... I was wondering if you were doing anything at the weekend?
    Well, I'm actually heading off to Cork. Why, what was the offer going to be?
    Nothing much – it was just that I had a spare ticket for the Neil Diamond concert.
    Well that's a real pity now.

Nobody told me what to do or say next. So, for what seemed like forever when it was probably only a minute, there was silence, then Eamonn piped up with 'I bet you feel like a right eejit now!' No sooner had he said that than I was cured. I no longer felt anything for him. The cheek of him, to think that I'd feel like an eejit! I was horrified. I came off the phone feeling like a new woman, liberated of all the feelings I ever had for this man. This was the first of many plunges that I took, some of which were successful and some of which weren't.
                                                  ANGELA, 28, A PRODUCTION WORKER

Aidan was delighted that I'd taken the plunge, as he'd fancied me for a few months, and now we're going out together.
                                                            FIONA, 24, A CLERK FROM CLARE

I asked Michael out after having fancied him for three months, only to find out that he was homosexual.   MONICA, 21

I got drunk – well, fairly merry – one night and approached a guy that I had fancied for ages. He was sitting on a high barstool in the corner, so basically he had no escape. I asked him what he thought of us getting together and he hummed and hawed until he eventually came out with 'I do like you, but I never thought this was how we'd get together. I mean... I thought it would be different. Look, what I'm trying to say is that I like you as a friend, but that's it.' No sooner had he said it than I just smacked him a smoochy kiss on the lips and I shot out of the night-club. There's nothing like a shock to sober up the system and, believe me, I was both shocked and sober in a split second. For the following two hours I bawled my eyes out, and would have been suicidal only for my friend's boyfriend, who spoke some sense to me. I kept whining on about making a show of myself, but he assured me that the guy would have forgotten all about it in the morning. Waking up the following morning was a nightmare. All I could think of was the previous night and the fact that I had practically thrown myself at a guy. For the next two weeks I kept thinking about it, but after that I was fine again. I told myself that this guy was not worth it, and that he obviously wasn't the right guy for me as he lacked the intelligence to see what an opportunity he had missed out on! I no longer fancied him, and was a cured woman. I've bumped into him a few times since but he just shies away from me, which pleases me because I realise just how shallow he is.

MARY, 23, A 'COMPUTER FREAK'

It makes sense to pick up the phone and just ask the lad straight out – why waste time sitting at home and wondering whether he is going to phone? OK, it can be upsetting sometimes to find out that he doesn't feel anything for you, but at least you can get on with your life.

DENISE, 23, A PRODUCTION WORKER FROM DUBLIN

I met a very nice, genuine chap at a party – he took my number, phoned me, and we met for a drink the following Wednesday night. It went really well – we had loads in common and I really liked him. However, days passed and there was no phone call. I had kept my weekend free in case he would phone. On Sunday night I was really peed off, so I took the bull by the horns and phoned him. He was shocked, and tried to make up some pathetic excuse why he hadn't phoned. By the end of the phone call I had managed to make him feel like a worthless low-life for not having the guts to phone me. I was delighted I had phoned him, and ever since I have been taking a forward approach, but, to be honest, I find that most men can't handle being approached by women. *This comment shocked me a little, considering the huge percentage of men who seem to have no problem with women asking them out. (It turned out that Fiona hangs out mainly in 'poser paradise' pubs and clubs.)* I work in the Financial Services Centre and tend to frequent the pubs nearby, which attract mainly bankers and other professionals.

VALERIE, 30, A BANKER FROM DUBLIN

Conclusion

Naturally, different pubs will attract different types of people. During the research I have visited hundreds of pubs all over the country, and found that the easiest-going, friendliest pubs are the most enjoyable ones. The 'poser paradise' pubs generally attract people who are caught up with their own appearance, and so busy looking at their reflection in the mirrors that they are not interested in anybody else. The majority of men who said they don't like being asked out by women were found in these pubs.

All in all, girls, it looks like hundreds of men are waiting to be asked out. So, go ahead and ask men out – there's loads to be gained from it. If the feelings are mutual then that's perfect, and if he doesn't feel the same way then you can be glad you know now, and not waste any more time on him.

We all know sincere guys who may not be the most confident when it comes to the opposite sex. It's just as daunting for them to ask women out as it is for us women to ask men out – it's not easy on any human being to approach another human being to ask for a date with the intention of developing a relationship if the date goes well. We don't know this person from Adam. In years gone by it was easier – there were arranged marriages, Ballrooms of Romance, etc. For us Single Individuals in the Nineties, it's not as easy as that. And judging by the positive responses I got from the men that I interviewed, it looks like a request from a girl to go on a date would make their day, and maybe even their night!

10 Sex – Too Much or Not Enough

Is é dúchas an chait an luch a mharú.
(It's the nature of the cat to kill the mouse.)

Let's face it – sex is the one topic that grabs people's attention. The media are obsessed with it because it sells newspapers and magazines. People are obsessed with knowing which film stars are doing it with whom, and how they do it. Sex and the discussion of it are far more open nowadays than 20 years ago.

Advertising is very sexual. Sexy men and sexy women sell products – take a look at the diet coke ad, or even the ad for the ESB. Women and men are being driven wild by billboards showing naked or semi-naked bodies. There are sexual stimuli everywhere you look. First thing in the morning when you hop on the train you will be greeted by Eva Herzigovina in her white bra, and last thing at night you'll have Calvin Klein boxer shorts stuck in your face. Even the clothes that younger people wear are getting skimpier. Is sex such a big thing, or is it all just media hype? Do men expect women to sleep with them on the first night? Do women expect sex on the first date? Who exactly carries condoms, and why?

The following questions were put to the interviewees. Would you ever have sex on the first date? Have you ever had sex on the first date? Do you carry condoms always, sometimes or never?

This is the one area where the figures don't add up, so there was either exaggeration or lying – you can decide for yourselves. Close to 90% of the 448 men who answered the question would not refuse sex on a first date, and as many as 46% have had sex on a first date, whereas only 19% of the 416 women who answered the question would have sex on a first date, but 28% admitted to having had sex on a first date!

The men who do

❝ I'd have no problem having sex on the first date. I enjoy sex, and it's a bonus when there's no strings attached. I've had first date sex about seven times, and it was very enjoyable. I always carry condoms. I'm not stupid. DECLAN, 33, AN INSURANCE BROKER FROM LIMERICK

I'll put it bluntly – no man on this planet is going to refuse sex on the first date if it was offered to him, just like very few women would refuse a diamond ring. Of course I'd have sex on the first date, but it's not usually on offer. There are times when I feel like a fuck. I don't want anything else. I've had first date sex twice in my life, and it was brilliant. One of the girls was foreign, so I didn't have to contend with the problem of bumping into her again. The other was a mistake, and I regret it still. DAVID, 32, A HORSE TRAINER FROM CORK.

Yes, I have had sex on the first date, a good few times in fact, but if a girl was willing to sleep with me the first time I met her, I hope she wouldn't expect me to phone her the following day because I'd have absolutely no interest. TIMMY, 28, FROM MEATH

Naturally, I've had sex on the first date. Sex on the first date, as in the first time you've met someone, is great physically, but emotionally it means zilch. You may as well be riding a blow-up plastic Barbie doll. ANDREW 33, A DESIGNER FROM DUBLIN

Men will be men. We're supposed to think about sex every 30 seconds. It's only natural, therefore, that we'll accept sex if and when we get the chance of it. If she's game, I'm always ready to shoot. PAUL, FROM ROSCOMMON, WHO WORKS WITH COMPUTERS

It satisfies a particular desire at the time, and it's fantastic and free. Nothing worse than bringing a woman away for a weekend or treating her to an expensive meal and not getting any physical thanks in return for it. Bit of a waste. *Is that why men treat women to dinner and weekends away?* It all depends on the type of woman. Take yourself as an example – I'd wine and dine you 'cause you seem like a bit of craic, but I wouldn't be expecting sex from you. Different courses for different horses, as they say.

JOE, 37, A FACTORY MANAGER FROM DUBLIN

Yes, I would have sex on the first date, and I have had once or twice. If more women said no, more men would have to do it themselves.

JACK, 26, A DRAUGHTSMAN FROM OFFALY

I think sex is very important. If a girl is frigid, I dump her. I don't see what the big deal is – when there are plenty of girls you can have first date sex with, why not? There's no point in wasting time and energy on iron knickers types. Life is too short.

DARREN, 23, A BOUNCER FROM DUBLIN

If it was an option, yes, most definitely, but it's not normally on the menu. The thing about sex is that in order to enjoy it, you need to know the person very well. To be able to discuss what you enjoy and don't enjoy. One-night stands and first date sex don't allow you to enjoy it. Fine for the 'wham, bam, thank you mam' type men, but it's a different kettle of fish for women. I don't honestly think women get as much satisfaction from it as men do.   TERRY, 35, A BUILDER

I only ever did the once, and that was on holidays. Having sex at the drop of a hat with numerous partners suits some people. They can cope with it and enjoy it. I'd say far more men than women do. Women are emotional creatures and need more than just a one-hour sex session in drunken circumstances. Some women claim to enjoy it and say that it doesn't invoke any slutty feelings – I find that very hard to believe.   BARRY, 31, A PLUMBER FROM DUBLIN

I've only ever had sex on the first date once. But I would like to add that, without a doubt, there are some girls who are just out to get laid. To begin with, they prance around in skimpy little tops and skirts and flash their eyes at every lad in the pub, and then ogle at you for a lift home – make that for a ride home!

DONAL, 34, AN AGRICULTURAL ADVISER FROM MEATH

First date sex is great. If the woman is game to explore and have a good time, all the better. I'd be selfish on a first date sex session. I'd get what I could and split. If the woman didn't enjoy it I wouldn't be bothered. With a girlfriend it is totally different – I'd do my best to please her. COLIN, 32, FROM CAVAN

I would never refuse sex on the first date – in fact, I'd be turned off a girl if she didn't agree with sex on the first date. I never carry condoms, and have had unprotected sex a good few times due to being drunk or just being surprised. HUGH, 24, A GRAPHIC ARTIST FROM CLARE

The men who don't

No, I'd always refuse. It's not my style. For me to be sexually involved with a girl, I would have to know her and feel comfortable with her. Having sex with somebody doesn't automatically mean that they love you or vice versa. Quite the opposite. If you love somebody you'll wait until you know them better.

PADDY, 30, A FARMER FROM WICKLOW

No, I've never slept with a woman on the first date – unfortunately, the opportunity never arose. Sex and self-respect go hand in hand. If somebody respects themselves enough and respects you enough they'll wait, and believe me, it's well worth it.

DERMOT, 29, A TAXI DRIVER FROM MAYO

I'm one of those very rare individuals who don't agree with sex before marriage. In fact, I find it difficult to discuss the subject.

GER, 38, A TEACHER FROM DERRY

There are far more important things to dating than sex. Sex is only great if there is a foundation there. Sex for the sake of it is not my cup of tea. I'd never have sex on the first date because I'd be too afraid of what I'd catch from a girl who was offering it.

CLAUDE, 27, FROM LIMERICK, WHO WORKS FOR MET EIREANN

I've never had sex on a first date, and I'd love to know where the women are that have sex on the first date. Have you got their

numbers? In all my hundreds of nights out with the lads and weekends away I've never had a girl phone me, ask me out or make a pass at me!
DERMOT, 37, A CHEF FROM KILDARE

It's sad to see the way sex is abused nowadays. And not for a second do I blame the men. You know what they say – it takes two to tango. The reason more and more men are expecting sex is because they're getting it. If people are out to get laid, they'll get laid. I never had sex the first time I met a girl, but I came very close.
MARTIN, A NURSE FROM DUBLIN

No, I wouldn't have sex on the first date. But I did once. We were on a stag night, and I blame the drink!
BILL, 29, A BUTCHER

It all depends – if I was cracked about a girl I'd never expect sex and would be very aware of the moves I make. I'd want to tread carefully for fear of losing her. I'd be willing to wait forever if I loved a girl.
JIM, 28, A FITNESS INSTRUCTOR FROM DUBLIN

Other comments from men on sex

I hope your book will answer me this question – what way do girls want us to treat them? Seriously, it's so fucking annoying. If you make a move on them you're a randy fucker, and if you don't you're frigid. What the fuck do they want?
DYLAN, 25, A COMPUTER ANALYST FROM WESTMEATH

It's so difficult to judge girls. Take this story as an example. I was out for dinner with a girl – it was the second date. The first time was in the night-club where we snogged. We had a great time, conversation was flowing and I got the vibes that she was keen. So I suggested that we go back to my place for a coffee. She agreed willingly. I had absolutely no intention of anything more than a snog and a hug. To save you being here until Easter, when I sat back down on the couch she practically jumped on me. I was shocked. It was the first time I'd ever had that experience and I genuinely didn't know how to react. I definitely think that I could have had sex with her but that wasn't what I was looking for. I did my best to explain that I liked her as a person and was interested in getting to know her a little better before going the whole way. She stormed out of my apartment, and when I phoned her the following day she wasn't in, *mar a dhea*.

SÉAMUS, 28, FROM KERRY

Casual sex and sex are two very different terms. Casual sex is where you shag somebody for the sake of it – there's no feeling involved. I've often ended up with girls that I called the wrong name, and that will just tell you how little it meant to me.

TOM, 29, A BUTCHER FROM CAVAN

It wouldn't be an issue for me to have sex on the first date, as in I wouldn't think twice about it. The closest I ever got to it was on the second, never the first – not yet, anyhow. I think it's nice when you try it on with a girl and you fail. It's a statement. There's no doubt that it increases your interest levels in her 200%! Men are the hunters in my view, and I like to call the shots. It's a challenge when a girl refuses to have sex with you. Jesus, that sounds awful. What I'm trying to say is that it's nice to meet a girl who hasn't and doesn't sleep around. When I get refused, I console myself with the thought that she likes me too much to sleep with me!

DIARMUID, 36, FROM CORK

I would think no less or no more of a girl if she didn't want to sleep with me. I went out with a girl for almost two years and we never had sex, yet we had a class A relationship. It has been my most enjoyable relationship to date. There's a lot more to life than sex. As for sex on the first date, it would mean nothing to me.

KEVIN, 34, A CARPENTER FROM CORK

Sex and respect go hand in hand. No guy wants to go out with a slapper. It's the age-old thing that most men would love to marry a virgin and all that. We want to sleep around and yet we want to settle with a clean girl. You can't have your cake and eat it. I'm often away with my job, and one night I was approached by a girl in the bar of the hotel where I was staying. I don't think sex would have been a problem, but it scared the living daylights out of me.

ANDY, 27, A SALES REP FROM GALWAY

Sex is an overused term nowadays. Everybody is far too obsessed with sex. It's sad, because the best things in life are free and so too should sex be. But there's a cost involved when sex is misused. What I'm trying to say is that when a lad meets a lassie at two or three in the morning and they end up naked in bed 60 minutes later, there is a price to pay. The cost is to your self-esteem. It cheapens an act which is supposed to be enjoyed by two people in love with each other. But this modern-day carry-on of hopping into bed with a different person every weekend will have a huge impact on one's level of self-worth. I've been deeply involved with women whom I didn't have sex with, and those relationships were no less meaningful than the sexual relationships I've had.

GARY, A MINER FROM OFFALY

As a barman I've seen loads of changes. Firstly, women drinking in pubs, which just didn't happen when I first started working. Secondly, years ago you'd just meet someone, go on a date and chat about how much land they had and get married. Today, people want more. Sex is so important, and particularly in a marriage – it's the foundation of a marriage, in my view. If you don't have that, why should you be with them? I see a huge amount of unhappily married men here, and it's disheartening. More people should stay single and play the field for as long as they can.

JIM, 41, A BARMAN FROM DUBLIN

Let's differentiate between sex and love-making. Sex is raw; love-making is tender. Sex is not emotional – it's the term used to describe the release of hormones between two people unknown to each other. Simple. Love-making, on the other hand, is a deeper act – no pun intended. It involves two people who are in love, participating in the most natural act on the universe. It's not embarrassing, dirty or, most importantly, regrettable.

TOM, 35, A SOCIAL WORKER FROM KILDARE

The women who do

❝ No problem – I'd have sex on the first date, but I only ever had on one occasion. JOAN, 31, FROM LIMERICK

One night I was in a club and this creature from heaven eyed me up all night long. When he asked me to dance, I just knew we'd have sex. There was a chemistry there. We bonded well, and it was the best sex I've ever had. Neither of us knew our second name but it didn't matter, it added to the whole seediness of the night. In fact, there wasn't much talking done that night. I've no regrets at all. I thoroughly enjoyed it and so did he. It's one of those nights that you only ever have one of in a lifetime.
CATHERINE, 31, A SECRETARY FROM DUBLIN

Of course I've slept with guys on the first date. There's no better feeling in the world than when you finally capture a man you've lusted after for ages. IRENE, 36, A FACTORY WORKER FROM DOWN

Yes, I'm ashamed to say that I have had sex with a man the first time I met him. If only you could bottle that deep desire for intimacy that you get with five bottles of beer on you – you'd make a fortune. ANNE, 31, FROM KERRY

I've had numerous first date sexual experiences. One in fact ended up being my partner for almost two years. It started one night after a disco – we were both fairly well oiled, and in the morning his father arrived home unexpectedly. We had such a laugh, because I had to spend the day hiding in his room.
PHILIPPA, 26, A PERFORMING ARTIST FROM CORK

I think if you plan to have sex, fine. It's a different ball game if you happen to have sex through drink or whatever. Then it has lost all its goodness. MARIANNE, 36, WHO WORKS IN A FABRIC SHOP

I suppose sex is so common today. Kids at twelve and thirteen are having sex, so that whole allure of getting someone into bed is gone.

It's no longer something that you can only get when married. It's freely available, so less and less people are frowning on women who have numerous sexual partners or who have sex at the drop of a hat. It's important to love the person. When you truly, deeply, madly love the person, it's the best pleasure in the world. Seedy sex is not as enjoyable at all. I'd carry a condom all the time on the off-chance that I might get lucky.
JOAN, 30, FROM WEXFORD

Yes – I don't see anything wrong with it. It doesn't do harm to anyone, and who has to know about it anyhow?
KATIE, 27, A MONTESSORI TEACHER

Sex with a stranger is brilliant – there are no emotional attachments and you can be selfish. I'm always very careful about being protected though.
CARINA, 29, A SOLICITOR FROM GALWAY

The women who don't

Personally, I would never have sex on the first date – it's not my scene.
CIARA, 23, FROM GALWAY

Never, and not on the second or third date either. For me, I'd have to know the guy well, feel comfortable with him and truly believe that the relationship had a future.
PAULINE, 24, FROM CLARE, WHO WORKS IN THE ARTS

Never had, and I never carry condoms. Sex is not the reason I meet men. Well and good if I get a shift and end up back in his place – I'd sleep with him as in share a bed with him, but I wouldn't have sex with him. One day when the right man comes along I'll go down that road, but not yet.
CINDY, 24, A COMPUTER PROGRAMMER FROM OFFALY

I've never had sex on a first date, but I have gone back to a lad's house and slept with him in the same bed with no sex. Sometimes you wake up the following morning and take a look at what's lying beside you and just die.
CELINE, 33, AN ESTATE AGENT FROM DUBLIN

No, not as in the whole way. I have slept with a couple of lads, usually when I've had a couple of drinks on me but not sex though. I'd only rarely carry condoms.   SINÉAD, 26, A HAIRDRESSER FROM KILKENNY

No, never on the first date. I'd have to know him. The notion that you are mature as soon as you start having sex with a boyfriend or girlfriend is wrong. At 19 or 20, you are dying to try it out but as you get older, you learn that there is an awful lot more to it.
KATHLEEN, 32, AN ADMINISTRATOR

No, I would never have sex on the first date. Most guys would try it on all right, and sometimes it takes a lot of willpower to resist, but it's well worth it at the end of the day. It's nice to think that they are interested in you sexually, but I suppose they're like that with all girls regardless of what they look like. Are they?
HELENA, 29, A TECHNICIAN FROM CLARE

Other comments from women on sex

At 3 a.m. going back to some chap's house seems like munna craic, but waking up the following morning is a nightmare. The amount of times I've woken up in strange men's beds is frightening. I wouldn't necessarily have had sex with them. It's great if he's still snoring his head off, because at least that gives you the time to remember where you are and plan a quick escape.
DOREEN, 33, A HAIRDRESSER FROM CORK

Far too many females think that sex is the be-all and end-all – it isn't. It's the best feeling in the world to work on a relationship and then sex comes along. Before that, it's not sex – it's pure selfish lustful reasons.   MAURA, 35, FROM WESTMEATH, WHO WORKS FOR A COMPUTER FIRM

There is nothing more upsetting than when a guy reckons he's in for the full works. They expect you to be ready. It's a complete nightmare.   MICHELLE, 31, A MIDWIFE FROM GALWAY

Sleeping with multiple partners on a regular basis is not a good thing. It cheapens the act of sex. You get what you accept, so if you lay every guy you meet you'll never find a guy to love or to love you.

FIONA, 29, A WAITRESS FROM KERRY

Guys try for sex the whole time – I even had a guy that I met at a dinner dance one night offer to marry me, just to see if that would change my mind about having sex with him.

JANE, 34, FROM CARLOW, WHO WORKS IN A PHARMACY

Years ago, men had to earn the right to sleep with a woman. They'd go through the motions of wining and dining first and then maybe sex would be on offer, but nowadays the cart is before the horse.

PAULINE, 33, A FACTORY WORKER FROM LEITRIM

I never had and never would have sex unless I knew the guy very well. I think sex has changed from being a subject that was always swept under the carpet to being a subject that is now happening on the carpet! It was wrong to treat sex the way it was in Ireland. Don't misunderstand me – the change that has taken place in our society in relation to sex in the late eighties and nineties has been too drastic. Nobody can cope with change overnight. The net effect has been that we have all gone overboard on the subject. It's not healthy. I personally hope that in time the transition from sex as being an unspoken dirty word to being a natural basic need will be melted into society the way it is in other European countries. And I hope it happens sooner rather than later, because it's far too over-rated.

MAURA, 31, A SALES REP

Sex is very important in a long-term relationship, but sex for the sake of it is all wrong. Sleeping with numerous partners is not healthy. In fact, it can be destructive to one's self-esteem.

DEIRDRE, 29, A CLERK FROM KILKENNY

It all depends – I had sex with a guy the first night we spent together. I was mad about him for ages and didn't want to let the opportunity pass. Unfortunately that's all it went on for, the one night. It's one of the great advantages of being single that you can have a varied and active sex life.

MAIREAD, 35, A CIVIL SERVANT FROM FERMANAGH

What makes me laugh is 'Are you coming in for a cup of coffee?' Everybody knows what a cup of coffee means. It would be more honest just to say 'Fancy some crumpet?'

TINA, 32, A QUALITY CONTROLLER FROM CORK

I'll tell you a funny story that happened to me once. I headed back to this guy's apartment one night for the infamous cup of coffee. As he had no kettle, he put a saucepan of water on to boil. At 6 a.m. the saucepan was black, as the water had evaporated.

ANNE, 26, A NURSE

It's sad to see society so caught up with sex. It's as if all young people are feeling obliged to have sex as soon as they have pubic hair. Sex is an adult issue and should be left to the adults. I never engage in intimacy unless I know the guy extremely well.

CLAIRE, 29, FROM DUBLIN

Carry condoms?

20% of men always carry condoms; 13% of women always do. 47% of men carry condoms sometimes, and 33% of men never carry condoms. 42% of women sometimes and 45% never carry condoms.

I'd never have unprotected sex – that's why I always carry condoms. It doesn't necessarily mean that I'm always having sex, unfortunately. If the opportunity arose, I'd be prepared though.

FRANK, 33, FROM DONEGAL, WHO WORKS IN THE MEAT TRADE

It's way too dangerous nowadays to have unprotected sex. I think AIDS did a lot to educate people on that subject.

AISHLING, 37, A TEACHER FROM KILKENNY

Depends – if I thought my chances were high of meeting a girl at a party or something I would definitely bring them with me.

PETER, 30, A CAR SALESMAN FROM DUBLIN

Nowadays, condoms are so freely available in toilets and shops etc. that it isn't always necessary to carry them – unless of course you have a favourite brand! MICHAEL, 35, WHO WORKS IN A MEAT FACTORY

I'm a single woman of the nineties, and yes, I always carry condoms. 'Prevention is better than cure' is my motto.

ANN MARIE, 28, A NURSE FROM KERRY

I've a condom in my pocket that my father gave me when I turned 21, and I still have it. I'm telling you, sex is not as freely available as you think. CORMAC, 24, A SOUND ENGINEER FROM SLIGO

Get real – it's the nineties; girls are just as bad as men if not worse. They carry condoms too, so what do you expect only sex?

PAUL, 35, A CIVIL SERVANT FROM DUBLIN

I've seen a change in recent years – women aren't half as gamey as they used to be. In the early nineties and late eighties it was never a problem to get unprotected sex, but now it's not so easy. I find more and more women are carrying condoms and aren't as willing to jump into bed. JOE, 37, A FACTORY MANAGER FROM DUBLIN

Yes, I have one in my pocket right now but it's a joke – we are on a hen night. I don't usually carry them.

LESLIE, 30, A BANKER FROM DONEGAL

It's a statement – 'Look, I've got condoms, so just let's enjoy ourselves'. Where's the harm in that? JOE, 28, A CARPENTER FROM TYRONE

If I'm out to enjoy myself and know there is a strong possibility of sex I'd carry them – I'm not ready for diseases or diapers yet.

YVONNE, 24, A RECEPTIONIST FROM GALWAY

Conclusion

Sex is a very personal issue and, as you can see, people's views on first date sex and condoms are varied. I think what is interesting is that so many men don't place as much emphasis on sex as women think. As Jim said, 'you can be absolutely crazy about somebody yet not be sleeping with them'. Personally, I hope that Irish society will lose its obsession with sex. It would be great if we had a more mature approach to sex like they have in other European countries. They treat sex with respect. Rather than being told that sex is dirty or sex is wrong, they are informed about its importance, its value and its consequences, and it is treated openly. Naturally, being human, when we are told not to do something we do the opposite. For example, if I tell you not to think of an elephant, what are you doing?!

11 The Funniest, Saddest, Most Interesting, Best and Worst Replies to the Questionnaire

Interviewee 1

Dick, who'd 'like to be known as Richard if the book ever gets published', is a 38-year-old army officer from Galway. He is separated and has no children, but 'as I'm not seeing anybody at the moment, I'm technically single for the purposes of your book'. He has spent time in the Lebanon and loves travelling in his spare time. He hasn't had a serious relationship in four years, and lives on his own.

Are you happy being single? Why?
Absolutely. It's the only way to be. I was engaged, married and separated in the space of one year, and it was a nightmare. I was only 24 at the time, and I literally fell like a monsoon rainfall for this girl who I met in a night-club at about 2 a.m. one night. We were both very drunk and ended up in her place. The following morning, I woke up in a single bed with the cheeks of my arse frozen stiff because she had taken all the bed clothes. We started seeing each other, and I thought it was the best thing in the world to have a woman who loved me. I know now that it was only lust. She was a great-looking girl and had a carefree attitude to life. She was four years older than me. A month later I proposed to her on the Eiffel Tower, and we married three months later. The marriage lasted all of five months and eight days. It was hell. As soon as she had me settled she was no longer interested in satisfying me sexually. I was crazy about her for seven months, but then I found out she was having an affair and I lost all respect for her. Since we split up 15 years ago, I have had a ball. This singles game is a marvellous experience. I can never see myself wanting to settle with just one woman

again. You're free to fly your wings and lay in whatever nest you find most satisfying, if you get my drift.

What attracts you to the opposite sex?
Child-bearing hips. They are such a huge turn-on for me – I adore them.

What is your favourite outfit on a woman?
Her birthday suit.

What are your pet hates regarding women?
Women who nag. When Hitler had Ireland on his hit list, Irish female nags had to have been his priority. I can't stand them. They are unhappy, ungrateful old hags.

Have you ever taken a girl's telephone number and not phoned her?
There's never any need for me to take a girl's phone number. If I want a woman, I'll go out, get her, end up in her place, shag her and just abscond in the morning with my trademark... if there's a lipstick hanging around I'll simply write 'see you later, sexpot' and leave. Women are hilarious. At three in the morning they're dying for it, but first thing in the morning they bury their head under the covers in disgust at what they've just done. It's great, 'cause you don't have to listen to the results of your performance!

Would you ever have sex on the first date?
All the time, if I can get it. I've slept with at least 50 women – I can't remember exactly how many of them were on the first date, but I'd say well over 20 were. I had sex for the first time when I was 14, with a 17-year-old woman. However, I will add that the best sex I ever had was with my wife, because I was more emotionally involved.

Do you carry condoms?
Always – doesn't necessarily mean that I'll use them, because if I'm not forced to, I won't. You know what they say – wearing a condom is a bit like washing your feet with your socks on.

What are your views on women asking men out?
I have no problem with it at all. I've been asked out a fair few times, and the first time it happens it's a thrill, but then it's just like anything else.

Have you any views on blind dates and dating agencies?
I'd have no need for them, as I'm well able to find a woman for myself without any help.

Best one-liner?
I would crawl three miles on broken glass in the freezing rain just to smell the tyre tracks of the laundry truck that takes your panties away.

What is love?
Does it exist?

Any other comments – things I may have overlooked?
I think women fall into one of the following categories.
- The fox – basically she is out to hunt and get all the lads chasing after her.
- The lizard – a slimy creature who has probably slept with your best friend but will deny it.
- The horse – a thoroughbred who looks great, has plenty of money and won't end up with a donkey!
- The hen – a nag. She'll hound you till your teeth fall out about carrying on the way you do, about always being late and about drinking too much.

Interviewee 2

Emma, from Dublin, is 31 years old and self-employed. She has travelled extensively for the past eight years. Emma has not had a serious relationship in almost two years, and lives on her own.

Are you happy being single? Why?
Yes, because I get to call the shots. I travel a lot with my job, so it's important for me to be able to get up and go without having to consider somebody else. Due to my erratic schedule, I need this freedom. I have a very varied and active social life. I don't think I would be as successful as I am now if I was involved in a relationship. I'd want to give a relationship 100%, and I haven't met someone that could support me emotionally in what I do as a businesswoman, i.e. wouldn't mind me going away etc.

What attracts you to the opposite sex?
There has to be chemistry. That doesn't mean they have to be good-looking – somebody who doesn't need to be needed, who's secure with themselves. A sense of humour is very important, because I like someone who is light, not someone who is heavy on life. Someone who would always look on the positive side of life and someone who would be able to satisfy my physical needs. He'd also have to like good food and wine!

It all depends what you are out for. If you're out for a good time, that's the type of chap you will go for – good laugh, dance, snog at the end of the night, you'll know if you like him. I don't like leading lads on – I'm not really out for just a shag. Never classify women as all women, or men as all men. Guys have a lot to answer for – there are some very genuine guys out there and there are some assholes. At the end of the day, the genuine girls will meet the genuine guys. Assholes will use and abuse you.

What is your favourite outfit on a man?
Casual clothes, jeans and a casual shirt, and I just adore chunky sweaters. I hate tracksuits on men and men in suits. A man looks more manly in casual clothes.

What are your pet hates regarding men?
I hate men who are macho or who want to be one of the lads. Pretentiousness. I don't have any time for men who don't understand women – men who are into self-gratification and don't know how to satisfy a woman's physical needs or even bother to find out. Cursing and smoking and excessive drinking.

Has a guy ever taken your telephone number and not phoned you?
I have only ever given my phone number on three occasions. They all rang and I dated all three of them. I have refused countless men my phone number because I wasn't interested or knew they wouldn't phone me. *How did you know they wouldn't phone?* Women's intuition.

Why do you think men take girls' phone numbers and don't phone?
Because they're not interested or it's an easy way out for them.

Would you ever have sex on the first date?
> I have had sex on a first date because I knew there was a high chance of it developing into a relationship, and it did. I don't agree with casual sex.

Do you carry condoms?
> I very rarely carry condoms. Only on the occasions when I know I'm going to be with someone whom I would want to have sex with.

What are your views on women asking men out?
> Fair play to them.

Have you any views on blind dates and dating agencies?
> Good idea, because you can be selective about what you want, and clear about who you want.

Best one-liner?
> A man has never used a one-liner on me.

What is love?
> A man who truly understands me and what I want. A man who'll be there for me 100%.

Any other comments – things I may have overlooked?
> I could go on forever without a man because I'm very happy. When I meet a man with the above qualities it will be the icing on the cake!

Interviewee 3

Scott is a 32-year-old who works in construction. He lives in a rented house in Waterford with three other lads, is mad about car racing and has been to Monaco and Australia for the Grands Prix. Has not had a serious relationship for three years.

Are you happy being single? Why?
> I wouldn't be any other way. I was engaged to a girl once for all of two months, and woke up one morning in bed with another woman and realised that I wasn't ready to get married, so I ended my engagement. It's the freedom – the ability to make up your own mind and not have to get permission to do things.

What attracts you to the opposite sex?
   Money – I love rich women.

What is your favourite outfit on a woman?
   A black swimsuit – topless, preferably.

What are your pet hates regarding women?
   Indecision. The older I get, the more disillusioned I become with them. Do any of them know what they want? Seriously, they have a language of their own. Think about it – when a woman says 'you look great', what she really means is 'I don't like that shirt'. 'I'm fine' means 'I'm bored stupid'. 'Of course I love you' means 'I'm not in love with you, you big eejit, I'm just using you to get at my ex-boyfriend'. 'No thanks, I wouldn't like another drink' means 'get me another drink or you're dead'. 'Don't send flowers to my office' means 'I'll kill you if you don't send flowers to my office'. And when they ask you if they look fat, you're supposed to start showering them with compliments about how great they look. 'The watch is lovely' means 'I wanted the solitaire diamond ring'. Worst of all is when they say they'd like a surprise for their birthday, so you do your best and consult all your friends for ideas, and finally when you hand her a pair of love-heart earrings she'll scream at you 'but that's not a surprise!' You can't win, honest to God – they all need a personal shrink!

Have you ever taken a girl's telephone number and not phoned her? Why?
   Too many times to remember – what else are men to do at the end of a night? Say 'thanks a million for the shift, I'd give it a five out of ten, now feck off home and dream about me?'

Would you ever have sex on the first date?
   I'm only human – of course I would.

Have you ever?
   Yes, twice – once when I was on holidays and once in the downstairs toilet of a girl's parents' house.

Do you carry condoms?
   Always. It's too risky nowadays not to.

What are your views on women asking men out?
　I only wish more women would do it.

Have you any views on blind dates and dating agencies?
　Not really.

Best one-liner?
　Would you like to get up on my crane?

Any other comments – things I may have overlooked?
　The world would be a better place if women didn't exist!

Interviewee 4

Ted is a 26-year-old from Donegal who works for the local dairy. He lives at home with his parents and is a keep-fit fanatic. Ted hasn't had a girlfriend since he finished his relationship with a girlfriend of two years, eight months ago.

Are you happy being single? Why not?
　Not really. I find it very hard to get used to the singles scene again. The pub and disco scene is a bit of a drag after a while. It's particularly hard when you're invited to weddings and family gatherings.

What attracts you to the opposite sex?
　Looks, personality and girls who don't wear a lot of make-up.

What is your favourite outfit on a woman?
　A school uniform.

What are your pet hates regarding women?
　Drunk girls falling around the place and puking.

Have you ever taken a girl's telephone number and not phoned her? Why?
　No, it's not my style to take a girl's number. If I'm serious about meeting her again, I'll make a definite date. In fact, taking telephone numbers is not really the done thing up here. Everyone knows everyone.

Would you ever have sex on the first date?
　Yes, if I got the opportunity, but it hasn't ever arisen... yet.

Do you carry condoms?
Very rarely. If I got lucky, I'd simply buy them in the jacks.

What are your views on women asking men out?
Do girls ask lads out?

Have you any views on blind dates and dating agencies?
I would associate them with lonely desperate individuals who had a serious personality or physical lacking.

Best one-liner?
I'll try anything once.

Any other comments – things I may have overlooked?
Meeting nice girls nowadays is getting harder and harder. I wish I hadn't given as much time to my girlfriend, because I lost a few friends over it and I don't blame them. It was totally selfish behaviour on my part. I don't think people are truly happy by themselves. Everybody needs a partner – people who say they don't are compromising. They are just justifying their single state. They might be only out of a bad relationship or something, but deep down people need people. Physical contact and intimacy are basic human needs.

Interviewee 5

Mary is a 25-year-old dental nurse from Kerry who shares a house with two girls and one fella. Her longest relationship was for six months, and that ended over a year ago. She has had only a few casual flings since then.

Are you happy being single? Why/Why not?
It's getting harder and harder. I suppose half and half – there are days when I hear my friends giving out about their boyfriends and I'm glad that I don't have one. But there is definitely a downside. Weddings, for some reason, are a real cringe factor – I suppose it has something to do with your subconscious, and wondering will it ever be you walking up the aisle. I think Valentine's Day is totally commercialised, and I never fall for commercialisation.

What attracts you to the opposite sex?
Looks-wise, I'd have to admit my weakness for redheads. Personality-wise, someone who keeps their distance. You need space in a relationship – if you haven't got space, you haven't got a relationship. I wouldn't go out just for a shag. The guy would have to mean something to me.

What is your favourite outfit on a man?
I love men in morning suits. For socialising, it would have to be jeans or chinos and a nice shirt or chunky sweater.

What are your pet hates regarding men?
V-neck sweaters and white polo necks – yuk. I can't stand men who smoke, or the poser types who love themselves.

Has a guy ever taken your telephone number and not phoned you?
Yes, lots of times.

Why do you think they do it?
I honestly don't know, and I can't understand it.

Would you ever have sex on the first date?
I would possibly have sex on the first date – I don't know how I would react in that situation, as it has never arisen. It depends whether I fancied him or not and whether I thought he was just out to use me.

Do you carry condoms?
No, never.

What are your views on women asking men out?
Personally, I would sit my driving test again in preference to asking a guy out – mainly due to the fear of rejection.

Have you any views on blind dates and dating agencies?
Only that I'd hate to think I had to resort to one to find a man.

Best one-liner?
I hate guys who use crude one-liners – in fact, I'm not really into one-liners at all. I don't think they work as far as girls with any bit of cop are concerned. But the best I did hear was 'Is that a ladder in your tights or just a stairway to heaven?'

What is love?
It's when two people idolise the ground they each walk on and trust each other 100%.

Any other comments – things I may have overlooked?
Well, seeing as we're discussing single people, I'd like you to make a note of the following. I think it's easier for a man to remain single than it is for a woman. The whole biological clock thing – it's infuriating. Even the term 'spinster' sounds so horrible – it's more like the name of a disease, whereas 'bachelor' doesn't sound half as bad. Could you please refer to single women as bachelorettes in your book? And finally, I hope your book will lead me to my Mr Perfect!

Interviewee 6

Patricia, 26, works as a machinist but has recently been laid off from her job. As a result, she had to move back to her parents' house in Waterford. Patricia has been single for almost a year.

Are you happy being single? Why not?
No, I'm not at all happy being single. I find it very difficult. I was going out with a guy for four years, and it's been over for almost a year now. Most of my friends are either married or going out seriously with somebody. And it's very lonely. I don't have anybody to go out with. One of the most annoying things is people asking me 'when are you going to give us a big day out?' It's a chore, and makes single life all the more difficult.

What attracts you to the opposite sex?
I like very good-looking, rich men. But they are impossible to find.

What is your favourite outfit on a man?
Calvin Klein boxers on a man who has a broad hairy chest and a tanned body.

What are your pet hates regarding men?
Men who go on about not having any money. It means you can't do

anything, and if you suggest going out for a meal, they'll choose the cheapest thing on the menu and make you feel guilty for at least a week for having suggested it.

Has a guy ever taken your telephone number and not phoned you?
Yes, I have given plenty of men my phone number and not a single one of them has phoned me.

Why do you think they don't phone?
I used to think it was because they lost it or something, but now I'm beginning to realise that they have no interest in anything but a shift.

Would you ever have sex on the first date?
Despite being out to have a good time and enjoy myself, no, I wouldn't have sex on the first date and I have refused more than once. As a blonde, men definitely think you are dumb. I think it has something to do with the Christian Brothers education where the men would have been taught by males only and hence they consider blonde women stupid. There are a lot of girls who may be overweight or not blessed with the best looks, and men use them for a good time. Men will call them jolly as opposed to fat, and expect to get their wicked way with them. It's tough on these girls who lack self-confidence, because they aren't strong enough to say no. Shifting or shagging different men on a regular basis is not good for your self-esteem. But we do have to get a 'service' every once in a while.

Do you carry condoms?
No, I don't need them. If I was having sex with a boyfriend I'd go on the pill.

What are your views on women asking men out?
A few of my friends have tried it, but the guys were not impressed. I personally wouldn't, but then again if this famine goes on for much longer I might have to!

Have you any views on blind dates and dating agencies?
Just that I wouldn't like to have to go to one.

Best one-liner?
I think they are the biggest load of rubbish. A bit like those pathetic sayings where there is always one to contradict it, like 'absence makes the heart grow fonder'/'out of sight out of mind'; 'opposites attract'/'great minds think alike' – they are stupid.

What is love?
To be able to adore a man always even if he had a tragic accident and was left disabled.

Any other comments – things I may have overlooked?
Sorry, but I'm a bit of a male-hater at the moment. At the end of the day, I think most men are wonderful. Hope that's OK, guys.

Interviewee 7

Max, 39, lives in Dublin and works as an insurance agent. He lived on mainland Europe for five years, returned home two years ago and hasn't had a serious relationship since.

Are you happy being single? Why/Why not?
I'm enjoying myself at the moment, but I would like to meet someone all the same. For the intimacy side of things and to share dreams with.

What attracts you to the opposite sex?
On a physical level, eyes. Eyes are the key to the soul – you can judge a person by their eyes. Women and men can even flirt with their eyes. I don't think enough people realise what a great asset eyes can be. Personality-wise, sense of humour is extremely important. I've a sense of humour and if somebody can't take a joke, there's problems straight away.

What is your favourite outfit on a woman?
Whatever shows off a figure the most. I suppose someone who's trampy but not over the top. The real trampy ones are the quick-fix types, nothing more. On a girl I liked, I'd have to go with a faded pair of tight jeans and a clean shirt. Tight jeans show off a figure if she has one.

What are your pet hates regarding women?
Jealousy. Where you can't be trusted. All men will eye up a good-looking woman, and obviously if this is noticed by your partner it can be blown out of all proportion. I would have no problem if a girlfriend of mine eyed up other men. I'd know that it was just harmless so there would be no need for me to get jealous. Trust is the most important thing in a relationship. It may be a small word, but it has huge role to play in relationships.

Have you ever taken a woman's telephone number and not phoned her? Why?
Because I was pissed and I didn't remember what she looked like the following morning. I'd have taken in the region of 30 or 40 numbers in my day. Initially, it's a bit of challenge to see if she would give it to you. Naturally, it's an ego boost if she does. If she didn't, fine; I'd think no more and just ask the girl standing beside her for hers. It all depends – if you wake up the following morning with a scrunched up piece of a cigarette box in your pocket and have to think 'what the fuck is this?', then obviously she didn't make an impression. If she was particularly good-looking then you would phone her. Initial eye contact will reveal whether she is a slapper or a sincere girl.

Would you ever have sex on the first date?
Yes, and I have had a good few times. You can meet the wrong people at discos. I wouldn't just pick up anybody. They would have to have something. If I was genuinely interested I wouldn't want sex or expect it. Some guys don't give a damn what she looks like as long as she's a woman. I've heard lads go on about all the women they've been with – the grannies, the young ones – it's crazy. It's all a counting game with some men, the 'notches on the belt' thing. One friend of mine slept with a 60-year-old one time, and it was absolutely disgusting to hear him going on about the gorey details. No morals whatsoever. Of course lads discuss the details of what they did with who, and how great or disastrous it was, but I firmly believe that decent men don't go on about it – especially lying about having slept with a girl. They'd be too afraid of getting caught out. In my day, sleeping with someone meant having sex, but it appears that there

is a whole new set of lingo now. Sleeping with someone doesn't necessarily mean that you had sex with them, which I find really bizarre. To me, it's just a pseudonym that non-virgins like to use to ease their conscience.

Do you carry condoms?

Always – they are always in my wallet – look! I remember about 20 years ago or so, a young lad joined the office. He was about 16 and was planning on having sex for the first time with his girlfriend, so he asked a few of us at tea one morning what he should do. Needless to say, we all told him that he had to go and get himself a packet of condoms as he didn't want to have a baby on his hands. In those days condoms weren't as freely available as they are today. The only place to get them was in the family planning centre in Merrion Square. It was well before the era of AIDS and all that. So, as he was going out the door I said to him 'You do realise that they come in three different sizes?' 'Really?', said he. 'Yeah – small, medium and large.' 'Oh', he said, so I asked him which one he was going to get. 'Medium, I suppose' was his reply. 'You'd want to be very careful, because if it's too big it will fall off and you'll be really fucked then.' 'Oh right,' says he – 'I better get the small one so.' Of course, we all had a right old laugh.

Have you any views on blind dates and dating agencies?

Well, I'd have to say that I don't know a lot about them, but from what I see in the papers, I don't think it would be something I'd pursue. Maybe it's the era I grew up in, but dating agencies were always for the spinsters and bachelors.

Best one-liner?

Chat-up lines are not something I would use. If I did, I'd probably get a reply like 'Jaysus, would you ever feck off'.

What is love?

Something inside that makes you all wobbly. Symptoms of love – you can't keep your mind off that person. Initial thing when you first feel that you've met the right person. Unfortunately, it fades away. Best sex is definitely with somebody that you are emotionally involved with – you can't define it.

Any other comments – things I may have overlooked?
I think finding someone you love is far more important than job, house, car, etc. It is definitely harder to meet people at discos and pubs nowadays. They're not the ideal place to meet – people are pissed, they're not in the frame of mind to make an opinion on someone. Next day, you are afraid because you can't remember what they look like. Also, there are huge numbers of married men hanging out in night-clubs. I can't understand it at all, especially when they are with single guys. I think both men and women are suspicious of that very fact – it's not healthy, in my view. I certainly wouldn't like if my wife went boogieing with single girls.

Pubs are for enjoyment, people out for the craic. If women are interested in fellas it's only for a one-night stand, because most men just go out to pick up a woman and it would only be for the night. I think you have a far greater chance of meeting someone through work or introduction. Consciously going out to look for someone doesn't work – it will happen out of the blue.

Wine is becoming more popular here, so maybe wine bars might be a thing of the future, but Irish pubs will always be there. European influence with the EU etc., might have a small effect also, but in the end of the day people will always go back to their local.

Interviewee 8

Catherine is a 34-year-old bisexual from Derry who works in the arts.

Are you happy being single? Why/Why not?
90% of the time, yes, I am happy.

What attracts you to the opposite/same sex?
Looks, sense of humour, dress sense, intelligence, shyness, music tastes and politics.

What is your favourite outfit on a woman/man?
   Levi's on both. Casual, androgynous, individuality. Not a fashion-victim mentality.

Has a guy ever taken your telephone number and not phoned you? And why do you think they do this?
   Because they are thoughtless bastards who like to give off a good impression, but they're probably not brave enough to phone when they're sober.

Would you ever have sex on the first date?
   I don't expect sex, but if the date was with someone I'd lusted after for a long time, I'd definitely go for it first time.

Do you carry condoms?
   Never.

What are your views on women asking men out?
   I have always made the first move – 98% success rate. Body language and other signals make it obvious that they are interested anyway, so why wait? Get in there!

Have you any views on blind dates and dating agencies?
   I think they are a great idea, especially if you are gay or bisexual.

What is love?
   Dependency, habit, selfish fulfilment, obsession, dreamy, scary, dangerous. Love is something different to everyone.

Any other comments – things I may have overlooked?
   Society dictates to people how they should behave, perform, etc., but if you're intelligent enough to realise that life is as good or as bad as you make it yourself and you are happy with yourself, then you'll be with people who enjoy being with you and you can learn to make the most of all relationships – not just personal ones. There could be questions about how you see society's expectations and whether you conform. Also, people's sexuality isn't explored, but maybe that's another questionnaire.

Interviewee 9

Thomas is a 29-year-old farmer from Sligo. He has never had a sexual relationship, and lives at home with his parents.

Are you happy being single? Why not?
No, I hate the process of trying to find a woman. I'm not getting any younger, and I'd like to be able to leave the land to a son like my father did with me.

What attracts you to the opposite sex?
Intelligence, sense of humour.

What is your favourite outfit on a woman?
Uniforms, be they white nurse's ones or garda ones.

What are your pet hates regarding women?
Smoking.

Have you ever taken a woman's telephone number and not phoned her?
Yes, I have taken one or two. It was the only way for me to escape.

Would you ever have sex on the first date?
I think I would be too nervous and shy and anyhow, the opportunity has never arisen.

Do you carry condoms?
No, never.

What are your views on women asking men out?
Brilliant idea – not enough girls do it.

Have you any views on blind dates and dating agencies?
I think it's a last-resort option.

Best one-liner?
I don't know any offhand.

What is love?
I don't honestly know, as I have never experienced it – I know what lust feels like though.

Any other comments – things I may have overlooked?

My big problem is that I'm only five feet five inches tall, which is a huge disadvantage for men. The average woman is the same height, so it automatically eliminates 50% of the girls at the disco or wherever. Society has unfounded beliefs that in order to be a real man, one has to be at least five feet eight or five feet nine, so it's a serious handicap for small men. Because discos are so visual in the sense that everybody is judged on what they are wearing or what they look like, guys like me don't really get a look in. Most women like to go out with guys who are taller than them or, at the very least, the same height. If you aren't a stunning woman or a handsome man that fits the classic cliché of tall blonde or tall, dark and handsome, you won't have much success at a night-club. It's all stereotyped.

When you're 18 to 25 you are happy enough with the disco scene, but after that you start exploring other social avenues like cinema and night classes. But even with the cinema it is very difficult to go there on your own. I'm a super-sensitive guy, probably because of my height, so I don't even enjoy going to the cinema with a male friend – it's stupid, I know, but I'm brainwashed into believing that cinema is for couples or a gang of girls, but not two lads on their own.

On the positive side, there is the likes of Van Morrison and Michelle Rocca – Michelle is a lot taller than Van, so it gives me hope.

Interviewee 10

Mick is a 27-year-old carpenter from Kerry. He has had numerous romances – 'some long, some short, but all enjoyable', and lives with his parents but is planning on buying a house 'as soon as Charlie gives me those tax breaks he promised!'

Are you happy being single? Why?

> Yes, I'm very happy being single. Take a box of Roses as an example – look what you would be missing out on if you never tried them all, especially the new ones they brought out last Christmas. Same with chicks – they are wonderful creatures, and it's great being able

to sample them all. And until I find the equivalent of the chocolate Rose in the purple wrapper – you know, the ones that have soft caramel in the centre wrapped in luscious chocolate, yum – I won't be settling.

What attracts you to the opposite sex?
How do you know I'm attracted to the opposite sex? I'm only joking. Everything that you have.

What is your favourite outfit on a woman?
An apron – I absolutely love women in aprons. Not that I want her tied to the kitchen sink or anything – well, not the whole time anyhow! I don't know what it is – it reminds me of those sexy chicks in the black-and-white movies who always wore them.

What are your pet hates regarding women?
Not being able to get the ones I want. Take yourself for example – I think that no matter how hard I try, I wouldn't manage to seduce you. You're one of those hard-to-tie-down types, aren't you?! I also hate woolly cardigans – the ones that give you the equivalent of beard rash when you are hugging a woman.

Have you ever taken a girl's telephone number and not phoned her?
Plenty of times. In a night-club, the music and a few jars put you in good spirits, you're feeling high on life and it's shifting for the sake of it. No serious interest in phoning them, but it's like an unwritten rule that you ask a girl for her number at the end of the night.

Would you ever have sex on the first date?
No. But I have done, unfortunately – it was a drink-related thing.

Do you carry condoms?
No, never.

What are your views on women asking men out?
More power to them – here's my number!

Have you any views on blind dates and dating agencies?
Not really, but if you ever join one let me know!

Best one-liner?
Why don't you leave that Dictaphone down and I'll put something in your hand that won't talk back to you?'

What is love?
The union of two souls – puke. In some cases, it's a disguise for dependence.

Any other comments – things I may have overlooked?
I'm not into the latest sex drive, where everyone is jumping into bed at a wink. Give me long slow painful romance and nervous touching etc., any day.

12. One-liners, Chat-up Lines and Quotes on Love and Marriage

The general feeling from both the men and the women is that one-liners don't work. 'Unless,' as Karen, a 26-year-old florist from Dublin, said, 'they are really funny and original. I hate those crude ones.' Men use them 'for a laugh', 'to get a reaction' or 'just for the hell of it'.

The old

- Do you want to dance?
- Do you come here often?
- Have I seen you here before?
- Fancy breaking a leg with me?
- How'd you like to be buried with my people?
- Do you mind if I stare at you up close instead of from across the room?
- Do you believe in love at first sight, or do I have to walk by again?
- I was sitting here holding a cigarette and realised I'd rather be holding you.
- Are you married or happy?
- How are ya fixed?
- Excuse me, but I think I dropped something – my jaw.
- I seem to have forgotten my phone number – can I have yours?
- What are you doing tomorrow?
- It's a question of mind over matter – if you don't mind, I don't matter.
- By God, but you're looking great tonight.
- You look like the type of girl who's heard every line in the book, so what's one more?

- What's your chat-up line, please?
- So, what are you doing for the rest of your life?
- Do you have a pen? Can you just write your phone number there please? (Pointing to his wrist – it always works!)
- I'd really like you to meet my mum.
- How would you be fixed for picking spuds tomorrow?
- Is it hot in here or is it just you?
- Are you hittin' the tiles?
- A guy takes ice out of his glass and crushes it on the floor, then says 'Now that we've broken the ice...'.
- I heard milk was good for your body but damn, you must drink gallons of the stuff!
- *Sheans a bi leat?* (any chance of being with you?) *(from Gweedore, Co. Donegal)*
- Hi, my name is John – how do you like me so far?
- If I wear your glasses, can I see you home?
- Is that a ladder in your tights or just a stairway to heaven?
- Your eyes are the same colour as my tractor.

The new

- Should I call you in the morning or nudge you?
- It's nice to meet you – I wonder what you'll give me for breakfast.
- You look confused, can I drink you a buy? *(think about it)*
- I don't bite unless you ask me to.
- What are the chances that we can engage in more than just conversation?
- Excuse me love, is that dress felt? *(No.)* Would you like it to be?
- Walk up to a girl's back and start fiddling with her collar. She will turn around and say 'hey, what are you doing?', to which you reply, 'checking to see if you were made in heaven'.
- Hand out cards that read 'smile if you want to sleep with me', and watch the girls try and hold back the grin.

- Are you free tonight or will it cost me?
- Can I buy you a drink or do you just want the money?
- I don't want to be alone when I go to bed tonight, but I do when I wake up!
- Stand still so I can pick you up.
- I'll try anything once.
- I'm fighting the urge to make you the happiest woman in this room tonight.
- Excuse me, are you wearing *Star Wars* underwear, 'cause your bum is out of this world.
- Hi, I've been watching you dance over there for a while and, to be honest, you're terrible – let me buy you a drink and we can talk about it.
- How about you and me have a party and invite your pants down?
- I wrote the *Kama Sutra*.
- That dress looks great on you, but I would look better.
- What nice legs you have – I wouldn't mind wearing them as a belt.
- If I gave you a negligee for your birthday, would there be anything in it for me?
- Did you know that your body is over 90% water and I'm really thirsty?
- Your place or mine?
- Hi, my name is Chance – do I have one?
- Take a seat – you must be tired, because you've been running around in my mind all day.
- Are you my real-life cousin?
- Let me talk you out of those wet clothes.
- Here's 20p – phone your mother and tell her you won't be coming home.
- Would you like to massage my sunburn?
- I'm emigrating to Australia next week.
- Since we shouldn't waste in this day and age, what do you say we use these condoms in my pocket?

- A guy rushes into a bar and interrupts a group of girls, looks at one of them and says 'Sorry I'm late'.
- Your teeth are like stars – they come out at night.
- Did you hurt yourself falling down from heaven?
- A guy approaches a girl in a bar and says 'I think you're very good-looking', but when he gets closer he changes it to 'well, I think you're good looking', so she says to him 'I think you're very honest – well, I think you're honest'.
- I'm new in town and I don't know the way to your house.
- Fancy me? Don't blame ya.
- How can you be so good-looking with just one head?
- Get your coat – you're picked.
- My lips are leaving in 20 minutes – be on them.
- Let's go to my place and do the things I'll tell everyone we did anyway.
- I'm sorry for staring at you, but I'm an artist and it's my job to stare at beautiful women.
- You're one in a million (she replies 'and so are your chances'!).
- If someone is into golf – 'do you play around?'

The borrowed

- Will we go so? *(Ballroom of Romance)*
- Why don't you come up some time and see me? (Mae West)
- I feel like Richard Gere because I'm standing next to you, pretty woman.
- Kiss me, big boy. (Marlene Dietrich)
- If I said you had a beautiful body, would you hold it against me? (Dr Hook)
- Is that a gun in your pocket or are you just glad to see me? (Mae West)

- I wish I was bisexual – it would increase my chances of being picked up on a Saturday night by 100%. (Woody Allen)
- There's only one boss in my house, and I do everything she tells me. (George Burns)
- The great question... which I have not been able to answer, despite my thirty years of research into the feminine soul, is 'What does a woman want?' (Sigmund Freud)
- Life is like a box of chocolates – you never know what you're going to get. (Forrest Gump)
- Kiss me, Hardy. (Admiral Nelson's last words)
- Lady Astor to Winston Churchill: 'If I were your wife, I'd poison your drink.' Churchill to Lady Astor: 'Madam, if you were my wife, I'd drink it.'
- My wife reminds me of the sea – not because she's dark, moving and romantic, but because she makes me sick. (W.C. Fields)
- Every time I get a good-looking woman, my wrist gets jealous. (Roy 'Chubby' Brown)

The blue

- Do you like gin and platonic, or do you prefer vodka and sofa?
- Sit on my lap, and we'll get things straight between us.
- I'd look good on you.
- I'm conducting a survey on how many people have pierced nipples.
- Your eyes are like spanners – when I look into them, my nuts tighten.
- Let's say your left leg is Christmas and your right leg is New Year's Day. Now, how about letting me get together with you between the holidays?
- That dress would look great on the floor next to my bed.
- Do you sleep on your stomach? *(No.)* Can I?
- Do you have a mirror in your back pocket? *(No, why?)* 'Cause I've been seeing myself in your pants all night.

- Let's go back to my place and get something straightened out.
- I don't mind if you're a lesbian – I've had female lovers too.
- Why don't you come over here and sit on my lap, and we'll talk about the first thing that pops up?
- I'd ask you up to dance if your tits were bigger. (She replies 'I'd have asked you first if your balls were bigger'.)
- The word is 'legs', so let's go back to your place and spread the word.

Some quotes on love and marriage

- Before marriage, a man will lie awake all night thinking about something you said. After marriage, he'll fall asleep before you finish saying it. (Helen Rowland)
- Wedlock – the deep, deep peace of the double bed after the hurly-burly of the chaise-longue. (Mrs Patrick Campbell)
- Courtship to marriage, as a very witty prologue to a very dull Play. (William Congreve)
- Happiness in marriage is entirely a matter of chance. (Jane Austen)
- Marriage is like a cage; one sees the birds outside desperate to get in, and those inside equally desperate to get out. (Michel de Montaigne)
- Love is being able to lie on a bed of stones with your girlfriend and still feel comfortable. (John, 25, a carpenter from Dublin)
- Love is an ocean of emotion surrounded by expense. (Pat, 23, from Clare)
- Come back next year and I'll tell you what love is. Because it will take me that long to figure it out. (Séamus, 32, a garda from Kilkenny)
- Love: one look can mean a thousand words. (Murt, 33, a fitness instructor and part-time bouncer from Donegal)
- A lady's imagination is very rapid; it jumps from admiration to love, from love to matrimony in a moment. (Jane Austen)

Conclusion

'I've been trying for hours just to think of what exactly to say; I thought I'd leave you with a letter or fiery speech like when an actor makes an exit at the end of a play.' (Meat Loaf, 'Read 'Em and Weep')

Well, what can I possibly say? If only I had known at 18 what I know now! I have learned a huge number of things from writing this book – most importantly, I will never ever give my phone number to a guy again, I will never ever go out to a pub or club with the intention of meeting a partner, and I will never write off any man, regardless of what he looks like, until I've spoken to him.

To the hundreds of really nice guys and girls who took the time to answer the questionnaire, a big thank you. To all the men who bought me drinks, a big thanks also, and to all the girls who were suspicious of me – I'm glad you can now see that it was a genuine chat-up! I hope the book has helped all of you who are unhappy being single to see that you are not alone. Maybe you are too caught up with trying to find Mr or Mrs Right. Try to relax and enjoy your singledom. To all the happy 'singletons', thank you for your insights. Marriage is a huge commitment – it's not a word; it's a sentence. Make it last. Do it for the right reasons, not because of pressure or panic about being 'left on the shelf'. Those of you who are happy in relationships, try to remember your single friends and give them a night out on the town every now and then.

I've spent two years in New York and one year in Paris, and all I can say is that my reasons for coming home were confirmed. Irish people are definitely different – they are real and whole and the majority of them are kind and caring individuals. Maybe some people just don't realise how much good they have in them. Enjoy life without doing any harm to those who love you or worrying those who care for you. Never forget that sometimes the heart feels what the eyes don't see.

I suppose I would never have written the book if I hadn't been single for the past three years. I enjoy being single 99% of the time, but every once in a while I miss the kisses and cuddles. I must admit, the day I got the news that my book was going to be published, I just wanted a six-foot hunk to wrap his arms around me and give me a big smoochy kiss. Unfortunately, that wasn't available.

There were three particularly notable features of my research. First, not one person refused to do an interview. Second, as someone who would previously have been attracted to a man's looks, my views have changed radically – some of the nicest guys I interviewed did not have the physical features that I would always have sought, yet I was sold on their personality and sense of humour. Third, NO – I didn't kiss any of the male interviewees, although I wouldn't have minded kissing quite a large percentage of them!

One of the best pieces of advice I can give you single folk is to buy a Dictaphone and go into a pub, club or shopping centre and start interviewing people on how they feel about being single in the nineties. It's the best chat-up line I've ever come across and, believe me, it works!

Finally, to Auntie Seppie – I hope I've taught you a lesson, and that you'll never again tell me to 'settle down'!